BORN AGAIN . . .

"Verily, verily, I say unto you,
Except a man be born again, he
cannot see the kingdom of God.

. . . Except a man be born of water
and of the Spirit, he cannot
enter into the kingdom of God.
That which is born of the flesh
is flesh; and that which is
born of the Spirit is spirit.

Marvel not that I said unto you,
You must be born again.

The wind blows where it will,
and you hear the sound of it,
but cannot tell from where it
comes and to where it goes;
so is everyone that is born
of Spirit."

— Jesus Christ
(John 3:3-8)

BORN
AGAIN
...and Again

How Reincarnation Occurs, Why
& What It Means to You!

by John Van Auken

Illustrated by Karen Kluge

**inner
vision**

Publishing Company

**1218 Eaglewood Drive
Virginia Beach, VA 23454**

This book is published by Inner Vision Publishing Co., Box 1117, Virginia Beach, VA 23451.
It is printed in the United States of America.

First Printing, Hardback Edition -- June 1984
First Printing, Paperback Edition -- June 1985
Second Printing, Paperback Edition -- June 1986
Third Printing, Paperback Edition -- January 1987

ISBN 0-917483-02-2

FOREWORD

As far back as I can remember I have been searching for answers to the inconsistencies and inequities of life. It always amazed me that so many of us live our lives without really knowing why life is the way it is. After years of studying, searching, questioning, I began to find some answers. They were not the answers I had expected but they were, nevertheless, the best, most logical answers I found.

Our narrow view of life beginning with birth and ending with death was the main reason life seemed so inconsistent and inequitable. These horizons of birth and death were just too narrow to allow us to see the whole picture. Within each of us is a level of consciousness, of life, that has been alive from the very beginning and will live on beyond our death. Soul is our truest form, not body and personality. Our souls contribute much to the circumstances and people in our lives, much that we fail to see, and this causes life to be so misunderstood.

This is my first book. It is the result of many lectures on the topics of reincarnation and karma. And, as you would expect, many, many people have contributed to it. It is intended to give a quick, clear overview of the story of reincarnation and karma, and to give you some tools for getting in touch with your soul's memories of past lives and their effects on your life today. I hope you find it useful and beneficial.

Table of Contents

PART ONE

THE MYSTERIES AND THEIR CAUSES

PART TWO

HOW TO FULFILL YOUR ULTIMATE PURPOSE

APPENDIX

IX

PART ONE

THE MYSTERIES AND THEIR CAUSES

Chapter One

THE BITTER-SWEET
MYSTERIES OF LIFE

I suppose all of us have reflected on what the true meaning of life is: Why do we exist? Where have we come from? Where are we going? Why do we live a life with so many memories, achievements, loves and growing understanding only to die and be separated from it all, or worse yet, to simply cease to exist? Could there be any purpose or reason behind the events we see around us and experience in our own lives? Are there answers to these difficult questions about life? Why is one child born handicapped, or into poverty, disease, oppression and an early death while another is born healthy and into comfort, opportunity and a long life? And who among us can hear news of an innocent person being brutally victimized by a total stranger and not wonder how there could possibly

1

be any rational sense to this? Why are some people starving to death in the world while others are
struggling to lose weight? How are these people
chosen? Is it all just some misfortune of nature, a
great big game of chance, luck? Or is there some
great plan behind all of this that we aren't aware
of?

Another puzzle to life is in the different
talents each of us are born with or without. Why
and how can a seven-year-old Mozart write a sym-
phony as well or better than men who have
studied music all their lives? Where does this
ability come from? How is one person chosen to
have it and another not?

Life's meaning and purpose is very much a
mystery to us, assuming of course that there is a
meaning and purpose. Something drives us to
want to find purpose and meaning, very few of us
live well without it. And yet, no one has completely discovered or revealed the whole picture hidden in the many pieces of this puzzle called life.

In the Western world there are two dominant sources for answers to these questions:
science and religion. Both try to unravel the mysteries of life. Both try to provide us with answers
to help explain the nature, origin, destiny and

purpose of our lives. To a limited extent they even try to explain the causes behind the circumstances of our lives—Why it is the way it is, why some of us succeed and some fail, why some suffer and others go merrily along.

Science builds its set of beliefs on observable, substantiated data. By its very nature science is centered around the observable universe, and for the most part it relies on the perceptive powers of the five senses and the enhancement of these with instruments. Beyond sensually observed phenomena it classifies most everything as theory. Reality according to science is what has been observed to be so and can be substantiated through physical tests.

The driving force behind science is the pursuit of knowledge. The mysteries can be solved if we learn how, why and what is behind the many things we see. Through investigation, study, hypotheses and testing, knowledge of all things can be obtained. With knowledge will come understanding, and with enough knowledge the entire mystery can be solved.

Yet science has done little to give meaning and purpose to an individual's life now. His descendents may come to know the meaning and

and purpose of life through the efforts of science, but there's little chance he will in his lifetime. Science works on a much longer time frame than man's eighty years. Religion on the other hand is quite different.

Religion's ideas are built upon centuries of human beliefs, feelings, thoughts and tenets. Its ideas do not need to be observed by the senses or substantiated by tests; they are accepted as true because a number of the religion's adherents believe it to be so. In most cases the validity of the leader's teachings and the tenets of the followers are accepted as true because they are deemed to be divinely inspired with the truth.

The predominant motivation for religion is the need to make sense out of death and suffering, and show a way to happiness. These beliefs are mostly centered around the need for a single individual to make sense out of his immediate life and to find a purpose in it.

The driving force behind religion is not knowledge; in fact, knowledge is seen as one of the causes of "original sin." For religion, faith brings one through the mysteries to the eventual understanding of life. The faithful will eventually know the truth.

4

Where science seeks knowledge, religion seeks faithfulness to the tenets already established. Where science gains through investigation, religion gains through living the tenets, and in some cases through inspiration and revelation. Where science uses reason and observation to identify truth, religion uses emotion and miraculous signs.

Let's look at the major beliefs in these two dominant sources of Western understanding:

Science defines life first in biological terms. Something is "alive" if it manifests certain biological conditions, namely: growth through metabolism, the ability to adapt to its environment through changes originating internally, and the ability to reproduce itself. By this definition a rock is not "alive" and an amoeba is.

Added to the biological quality of being "alive" science identifies levels of "aliveness"— an amoeba may well be alive but its level of awareness or consciousness in no way compares with that of an ape. The ape is more alive because it is not only biologically living through metabolism, reproduction, and internally adjusting adaptation, but it is also *perceiving* more of its inner and outer environment. It displays the conditions of having attitudes, emotions and memories, as well as the powers of thinking, learning and communicating.

When science looks around the observable world it sees gradations of "aliveness" from the merely biological to the highly conscious forms of life, and it sees evidence that these gradations have evolved from the simple to the complex over long periods of time. At present science finds enough evidence to propose that the origin of human life was a fortuitous event in the waters of this planet millions of years ago in which circumstances were just right for the emergence of biological life in its simplest form, and that this life has evolved to the level we possess today.

Science's view of life, though contributing to the overall picture of the processes involved in life, does not give much meaning to an individual life. As of yet, science finds no apparent purpose to life other than the perfection of the species through "survival of the fittest." One's life is just a result of the forces of nature.

An individual seeking answers, reasons and meaning to his or her life finds that it can be scientifically described as little more than the result of the random contact of one single sperm cell (out of millions of sperm cells) with one egg, and the subsequent division of these cells. This group of cells called our body will live for about 70 or 80 years if it isn't destroyed by disease or some unfortunate incident, and will then stop living. Its species will go on perfecting the life-form through the genes it passes on through reproduction carrying the codes of form, adaptability, metabolism, and reproduction.

For the individual, science can contribute only to the quality of his or her life now, but beyond this life it gives little hope. Death is the end of life for the individual. New beings will rise up, live in their glory, pass on their genes and then decay and die. Perhaps sometime in the future science will discover a way for individuals to live much longer or even indefinitely, but now they will die. And even if science learns how to prolong life there is no evidence it will provide a purpose or meaning to life.

Religion teaches that all life was created by a divine being. And even though the deity's ways are mysterious for man to understand, they are purposeful and have meaning.

In religion's beliefs man is God's greatest creation. The individual human being is more than a biological organism, it is a "soul" or "spirit" which lives beyond biological death. In this way the life of an individual is not lost at death but goes on. All its achievements, joys, loves, and memories are not ended, but actually contribute to the individual's life beyond death. According to religion man has the opportunity to live forever with God in heaven after his earthly life ends.

The reason earthly life has suffering and disappointments is twofold: 1) Original Sin. This is the result of a sin committed by man's ancestors, Adam and Eve. According to Western religion they were the first man and woman to be created and from whom all others have come. These two lived with God in the Garden of Eden and walked with Him daily. But they ate a forbidden fruit from "the tree of the knowledge of good and evil" and for this offense they were banished from the garden and the company of God, and all men and women that came after them have a much harder life because of their sin.

2) The second reason for suffering and disappointment is misuse of one's own free will. Whenever one's will crosses the will of God the individual experiences discomfort, suffering

and disappointment. Another part of this concept is the idea that a person learns from suffering. Therefore, a person sometimes experiences suffering not because of their actions but because they need to learn something.

Religion also holds that a person's biological life on earth is an opportunity to live according to a code of moral and behavioral guidelines in such a way as to earn the privilege to enter into heaven after death and live with God in spirit. Heaven is the home of the divine creator and is a joyous place to abide.

If one does *not* do well according to the moral and behavioral codes he will enter one of two other places, depending on which religious sect one belongs to — purgatory and/or hell. In purgatory his soul suffers hard for its sins but as the name implies it is eventually freed to enter heaven after it's purged of evil. If, however, its sins are too grievous the soul enters hell forever. Here it suffers excruciating pain without end.

Even though religion tries to provide man with the meaning and purpose of life, it leaves many important questions unanswered, and in some cases its tenets create more questions. Questions like: If this life is an opportunity to live in such a way as to earn the privilege to enter heaven, why then are we all not given the same opportunity to live this life well? Why are some souls born into environments of crime and sin while others are born into more constructive environments? Why are some of us born blind, crippled or with a terrible disease? Why are some of us robbed, raped, murdered, and so on? Why are some of us born into areas where the tenets of the religion aren't even known? And, why does God create a soul who has no choice in the matter of his coming into being, only to eternally punish him severely because he didn't live up to the code required?

Science and Religion contribute much to our lives and each has some of the pieces to the puzzle of life, but neither has been able to explain life completely.

THE SECRET TEACHINGS

There is a third source for answers to the mystery of life. It's not as organized and well defined as science and religion, but its explanations hold together so well and are so comprehensive that one should seriously consider it.

Unfortunately, this source has no unifying name to its body of knowledge. Various parts of its principal concepts are actually scattered throughout different cultures and countries with no clear central collection point for its ideas. Because of this, and because many of its ideas are not widely known, and often the adherents of these ideas have closely guarded them from the public, and for lack of a better name I'll refer to this school of thought as "Secret Teachings."

Science might catagorize the Secret Teachings as "metaphysical," meaning beyond the known laws and observations of physics. Religion would refer to them as "mystical," meaning that they belong to a collection of thought considered to be too mysterious to consider or of dubious origin.

In the following chapters the Secret Teachings will be described in as much detail as I can gather together from the many different sources for these ideas. And perhaps you will find, as I have, that the Secret Teachings possess an unusually comprehensive view of life and answer many of the questions we've all considered so unanswerable.

In order to understand life as it is seen by the

Secret Teachings we have to go back to the story
of the original creation and retell it because the
way we have it today is not quite correct.

Here is the story of the original creation,
with all of its purposes and influences in our lives
today, according to the Secret Teachings.

Chapter Two
THE SECRET GENESIS

Imagine the universe *before* the beginning, before anything existed. Visualize the vast emptiness of absolutely *nothing* for as far as you can see in any direction. Nothing exists. Yet, despite the emptiness it is alive. The force that will eventually begin the creation is there. This empty, silent, dark eternity is actually the *consciousness* of the creator before it begins the creation. It is very much alive, but still and quiet, like a consciousness without a thought — aware, perceiving, but not conceiving, thinking or creating.

Then, at some moment in this timeless void the consciousness moves. Something deep within itself stirs from its stillness and begins to awaken and express itself in thought, images, light and sound. The creation has begun. The great silence has ended and the universal consciousness has begun to conceive, imagine and express itself. Within the void light appears, eventually stars and galaxies appear, and on, and on.

However, none of this was *physical form*. The "form" was like an *idea* in the consciousness of the creator. It was the essence of a star, the mental concept of a star, not the physical form — only the idea of a star. And as hard as it is for us to imagine, the idea of a star is its *true* nature. The form we have become so familiar with is only the physical manifestation of the star's true nature.

The original creation occurred in the consciousness of the creator and the creations were like ideas, only later did they take form.

The creative expression was wonderful, harmonious and filled with vitality and life, but for the creator there was something yet to come. According to the Secret Teachings the creator wanted to share this expression of life with others who could appreciate it and find fulfillment within it. Because of this desire, and for this purpose the creator conceived of a very unique creation: *companions* — individual points of independent consciousness just like itself. They would be able to perceive, conceive, express themselves and re-member. But most of all, they would be able to directly communicate with the creator, knowing its nature and thoughts, and sharing their own.

It was truly a marvelous conception, but it had one potential flaw. In order for the com-panions to be true companions they would have to be free to *choose* to be so, otherwise they would merely be servants and automatons of the crea-tor's will. Yet, if they were given independent wills of their own they might choose *not* to be companions and would become like a runaway cancer in the consciousness of the creator.

However unpleasant this possibility was, the benefits of sharing and experiencing the creation with others and seeing their conscious-nesses unfold and expand was worth the risk of a possible rebellion. But, to insure that the Whole would survive any rebellion a Universal Law was set: For every free-willed action by a companion there would be a similar *reaction* upon the com-panion. In this way everyone would have to live with the effects of their use of the gift of con-sciousness and free will. When the actions of a companion were harmonious, harmony would be a part of the companion's experience, but when

15

the actions were rebellious (in other words, self-glorifying, self-gratifying, self-centered, and without regard for the Whole) then the companion would experience the effects of rebellion—each must experience the effects that their actions have caused.

Interestingly, science and religion recognize this law. In science it is often stated as, "For every action there is an equal and opposite reaction." And in religion it is, "An eye for an eye, a tooth for a tooth," "As you sow, so shall you reap," and "As you do unto others it will be done unto you."

Once this law was established the creator conceived and freed countless independent points of consciousness within its own infinite consciousness and the companions came into being, each conscious and free. Each had the ability to perceive, conceive, imagine, create and remember. What a trembling wonder it must have been in those first moments.

It's important to realize that the companions were not physical bodies. They too were like "ideas" in the mind of the creator that were given freedom to be independently conscious. As they used their freedom they developed into unique

16

points of thought, feeling, desire, expression and memory. Each was slightly different from the other by virtue of their different vantage point within the universal consciousness and by the different ways they each acted and reacted to their new consciousness, to their new freedom and to life around and within themselves. They were developing ideas, becoming clearer and more uniquely defined and identifiable as they experienced life, but like an idea, they were not three-dimensional form. Their true "form" was consciousness. Life in its most human-like nature is consciousness.

This is why it would be very difficult for science to observe the whole truth about life. It is too focused on the physical, observable world of the third dimension, and it will not easily understand the *essence* of life as long as it continues to study only the manifestions of life.

According to the Secret Teachings the companions were also androgynous, having both male and female qualities in one being. It was only later when they entered the strange duality of earth that the two aspects of the individual were separated.* We'll get into this in more detail in chapter three.

The companions' nature can be further broken down using terms we are familiar with today: SPIRIT is the essence of life itself. The difference between something being dead or alive is the presence or absence of Spirit. Spirit is life. The condition of the creator before the creation is Spirit, pure life, alive yet still. Life in motion, or the power to move and shape ideas and even forms out of life is MIND. Mind is the sculptor, the builder who conceives, imagines and shapes ideas out of the essence of life. Spirit is life, Mind is the power to use it.

Each of the companions has Spirit and Mind, but each experiences life a little differently, and these different memories build a unique individual. This individual aspect of the companion is SOUL. Soul is the sum total of all the companion has done with its free-willed consciousness. Soul is the companion's story,

*Our language has a severe handicap in its inability to allow for a neutral pronoun, forcing one to use "he" when one actually means "he or she." In some cases you'll see that I've used "it" or "its" as a pronoun for companions and the creator. In other cases I'm forced to use "he" because I don't want to imply a non-personal quality to the companions or the creator. But unless I clearly state otherwise, when I use "he" I mean "he or she."

its complex of memories that result from all it has seen and done. All of the companions have Spirit and Mind but each has a different Soul, because each has a different collection of memories and experiences, different desires, hopes and attitudes about life. As you can see, the soul develops. It changes as the individual lives and experiences life and gradually builds its own collection of memories which result in opinions, ideas and viewpoints. Spirit is the life force, Mind is the power to use it and Soul is the being that develops. All are one in consciousness.

INTO THE EARTH

The companions, filled with their new found consciousness and freedom, went out into the vast universe to experience life and to learn about themselves, the creator and their relationship to it. In their travels through the cosmos some of the companions came down into the third-dimensional influences of the planet Earth where they entered into physical form for the first time. Here they became so enthralled with the physical that they began to identify themselves with their forms. They began to think of themselves as physical entities, rather than free, living consciousnesses. Incredibly, these celestial beings began to think they were truly terrestrial beings only! Form was so substantial, so captivating that it was difficult to hold onto the more delicate reality of consciousness.

The inevitable result of this strong identification with the physical was that it was subject to the laws of nature, and therefore it had a cycle of its own and a part of that cycle was death. The body would come to life according to the laws of nature, live for a time and then die. In their original state the companions were continually alive, but those that began to strongly identify with their physical bodies as being themselves were now affected by death. If they thought they were their bodies, then when their bodies died they thought they died. And for all intents and purposes they *were* dead. "As the mind thinketh, so it is."

This was a serious confusion and when the companions who had *not* become involved in the earth saw what had happened to the others they decided to help them regain their former state.

However, it was not going to be easy. The earth-bound companions had continued in this masquerade for so long they were deeply possessed by the belief that the physical world was the real world, even to the point that all else seemed like phantoms and dreams. Life for them had become totally biological. Before their physical parents joined together to make their physical body they were "just a gleam in their daddy's eye" and if they were lucky, they'd live a long physical life, but eventually die like all those that had come before them. That's as far as they could see. Life was totally physical.

In addition to the influences of the physical dimension, the souls were building reaction patterns with their willful activities in the physical world. According to universal law these actions had to be met, and the only place they could be properly met was in the physical where they had been initiated. So the web was becoming more and more tangled and complex. The more one acted in the earth, the more one built earth-debts that had to be met in future earth-reactions. There were going to be no quick outs for anyone. Once a soul touched the physical, it was certain to become possessed and confused

21

by the very nature of the realm and the longer it lived in the earth plane, the more it built patterns that would have to be met. The process would be long, hard and not without great sorrows, for as long as the physical life was seen as the real life the companions would experience pain, disease, loneliness and death. The only joys found in the physical would be those of the Spirit and these would be so delicate or intangible in the physical world that it would be difficult to hold onto them, not impossible, but difficult.

Another effect of entering the earth plane was the separation of consciousness. As an individual entered deeper into the physical its consciousness separated into three areas of awareness: The physical world and the human body required a three-dimensional consciousness that could function in the earth. We call it the *conscious* mind. It has become the part of our consciousness that we are most familiar with, many of us would consider it to actually be the "I" or "me" of ourselves. It is with this part of consciousness we experience physical life and our personality is developed. In many ways it is our earth-self.

The second part of awareness is subdued

22

LEVELS OF CONSCIOUSNESS

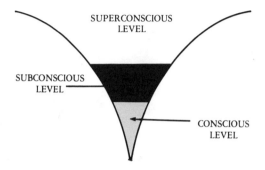

SUPERCONSCIOUS
LEVEL

SUBCONSCIOUS
LEVEL

CONSCIOUS
LEVEL

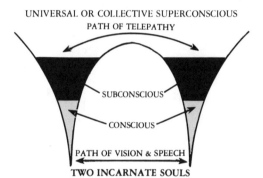

UNIVERSAL OR COLLECTIVE SUPERCONSCIOUS
PATH OF TELEPATHY

SUBCONSCIOUS

CONSCIOUS

PATH OF VISION & SPEECH
TWO INCARNATE SOULS

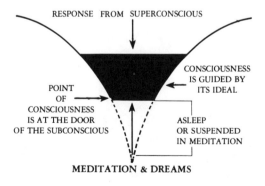

RESPONSE FROM SUPERCONSCIOUS

CONSCIOUSNESS
IS GUIDED BY
ITS IDEAL

POINT
OF
CONSCIOUSNESS
IS AT THE DOOR
OF THE SUBCONSCIOUS

ASLEEP
OR SUSPENDED
IN MEDITATION

MEDITATION & DREAMS

Note: These diagrams were first shown to me by Dr. Herbert Puryear at the A.R.E.   As far as I know he first conceived them.

and shadow-like while one is incarnate. It lives life like a shadow, always there listening, watching, remembering and only occasionally does it make its presence known, but those times are profound, sometimes frightening. This part of consciousness is similar to what we call today, the *subconscious*. From out of this area come sleep dreams, intuitions, unseen motivations, and deepest memories. The subconscious is the realm of the developing soul and it uses the conscious mind as a mechanism for manifesting in the physical plane through the five senses. Often the conscious mind combined with the desires of the body becomes so strong and dominant that only its activities seem important and real, the subconscious seems illusionary. But in truth, the real life is occurring in the subconscious.

The third area of the now divided consciousness is the most universal. It is the part that can perceive and commune with the consciousness of the creator. We can call this the *superconscious.*

As this diagram illustrates the more one's attention moves into the conscious mind the more narrow and limited the focus and aware-

ness. The more one moves toward the superconscious the more one becomes aware of the
Whole, the Universal Forces, the Creator.

It may be more difficult to perceive the
infinite when one is so grossly involved in the
finite, but the universal consciousness of the
creator and the potential for attuning oneself to it
remains accessible. In time the earthbound companions could become aware of the difference
between terrestrial life and celestial. They could
come to know their original state and purpose
and regain their celestial birthright of companionship with the creator. In time they could
come to realize that the conditions in their
present physical life are a result of their free-
will actions and choices before this life.

They could even come to know again that
they are co-creators with the creator of all and
were with Him in the beginning.

When the earthbound souls genuinely begin
to believe that the physical cannot possibly be
all there is to life, they can begin the long journey
back from manifested form to spiritual consciousness, a very difficult journey. One cannot
think one is a lump of flesh, blood and bone and
expect to instantly drop this idea and easily pick

up another more ethereal idea. The influences of finite form on an infinite being are profoundly stupefying and it takes patience and commitment to shake off these influences and fly free again.

Now many of the celestial beings created to be the very companions of the creator of all the universe are far away from home, lost in a world with many distractions and illusions. Surprisingly, the lost ones don't even think they're lost. They have accepted a totally new reality, while the creator and the other companions contemplate the situation in hopes of finding a method for rescuing these lost ones.

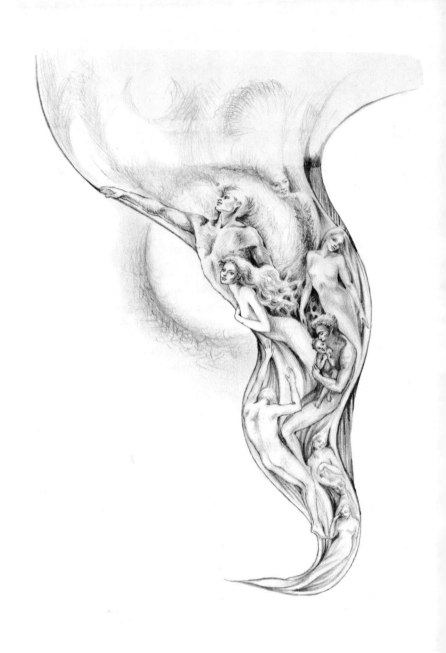

Chapter Three

TO THE RESCUE!

The souls near the earth but not involved in it were in a position to help the earthbound souls. At first they entered straight into the earth to help reawaken the others, but when they found themselves becoming distracted, confused and captivated by manifesting in form they wisely decided to regroup and reconsider more carefully how they might achieve a rescue. It quickly became apparent that the physical dimension was a far more difficult problem than anyone had at first imagined. No matter how good one's intentions once the transition from soul-in-consciousness to soul-in-substance was made, it was nearly impossible to retain an awareness of one's true nature. Substance was too consuming, and you couldn't just touch it and then leave it

27

alone. To use an old southern concept, it was like grabbing hold of a tar baby—once you touched it, it had a hold of you.

In some ways entering physical form can be compared to entering a costume ball. In order to get in you have to put on a costume, and once in costume you and those around you begin to think of each other as being the image of the costumes. After playing this game long enough, you become so familiar with the costume reality that it becomes the dominant reality. You forget everyone is really a person in a costume. And, of course, to add to the confusion the ball is very exciting, filled with lights, music, foods of all kinds, dancing and activities galore! Your entire focus becomes the ball, the costumes, the adventure, and the party goes on forever. But the longer you stay the more your costume wears away, until it is worn thin and the seams give way and you can't use it any longer. Without a costume you have to leave. If you want to return you must find another costume and then you can enter the party again. Before you know it, everything revolves around the ball and your efforts to stay at the ball or return to it with a new costume. Everyone has forgotten that within the bodies are real souls and beyond the physical world is an entire spiritual universe and a creator who wants to share it with them.

Helping the souls at the "costume-ball" was not going to be easy. They were now so focused on the ball and the costumes that they could only be communicated with *at* the ball and *in* costume. The rescuing souls were going to have to risk getting themselves lost in order to communicate with the others. Ultimately all the souls that touched the physical would have to experience the separation of consciousness and the blinding limitations of three-dimensional reality and then somehow overcome it! There was simply no easy way in and out; one had to come to terms with it until no longer possessed by it, but it was just one dimension out of many in the consciousness of the creator.

To protect against the loss of the truth completely, the rescuing souls wove the truth about the companions and their predicament into the fabric of physical life, into its legends and myths, its art and symbols. Then, when any lost soul sought beyond what he found in physical life, the real truth would be there for him.

29

BORN AGAIN AND AGAIN

Three famous examples of these secret-meaning tales are Sleeping Beauty, Snow White and Pinocchio. Each of these compelling tales has a theme based on the battle between good and evil for possession of an innocent person who wants only to live happily ever after. Despite all efforts to prevent it, the innocent one is killed by evil, but eventually he or she comes to life again through the forces of good and experiences the full measure of his or her dreams.

In Sleeping Beauty's tale her marriage to the prince was doomed when she pricked her finger on a spinning wheel and died, but the penalty was reduced to "a deep sleep." Through the prince's efforts to free himself from the grips of evil and defeat the dragon he is able to reach Sleeping Beauty and awaken her.

In Snow White's tale her marriage to the prince is lost because she eats the apple that evil presented to her and dies, but she is really not dead, only in a deep sleep. After searching long and hard the prince finally finds her deep in the forest and awakens her with a kiss.

In Pinocchio's tale we find a wooden boy who can become a real boy if he proves himself worthy. In his efforts to live the way he should

Pinocchio falls prey to many of evil's distractions; each has a devastating effect on him, and the last challenge kills him. But because he was trying to save Geppetto's life rather than his own in those final minutes of life, he is granted the promise of the good fairy and comes alive again as a real boy.

In the tales of Sleeping Beauty and Snow White the soul of a companion is symbolized by the beautiful, innocent princess. The prince symbolizes the mind of the companion. He is the companion's power to reason, understand and perceive so that he can cut through the illusionary powers and darkness of evil and reunite with his soul. It is the light of understanding that shines through the darkness and reveals the truth. In these two tales the mind had to struggle with many powerful illusions, especially in the story of Sleeping Beauty.

Sleeping Beauty's loss of consciousness by pricking her finger while she was spinning on her spinning wheel is symbolic of the soul's entry into flesh and blood through the use of its free will (spinning its pattern). The evil fairy who predicts the coming doom and eventually grows into the fiery dragon and challenges the mind's efforts to revive the soul is the evil of self—self-glorification, self-aggrandizement, self-centeredness, and self-willfulness; all to the detriment of the Whole.

We see this same evil power personified in the Stepmother-Queen of Snow White. "Mirror, mirror on the wall who's the fairest of them all?" As we will see later in the legend of the Fallen Angels this self-centered vanity is a major stumbling block to independent consciousness and free will.

In Pinocchio we have an even clearer picture of the companion's struggle. The individual cannot become a real companion and share the full meaning of companionship with his father (who created him) until he comes to terms with his freedom to choose. But his conscience can show him the way, and concern for others is a major step in recovering from misuse of free will.

There are many fairy tales, myths and legends containing elements of the story of the companions. Inevitably they become the favorites.

Another is the Wizard of Oz. In this story the soul, as Dorothy, finds herself in a strange land far from home. In her quest to get back home she meets three aspects of herself that are lacking something: heart (the tinman), mind (the scarecrow) and control or courage (the lion). By following the path and after many trials she arrives at the Wizard's castle only to find that the way home was within her all the time. So it is with the companions of God who are in the earth.

Another that we should consider before we move on is the legend of the Fallen Angels. In this legend we find the basic theme again, but with a curious twist:

"In heaven there was an angel of such beauty and brilliance that he was called, 'The Morning Star.' His real name was Lucifer. Lucifer began to think only of himself. He was so beautiful and independent that he felt he needn't cooperate with anyone, even God himself, Lucifer's creator. He began to do as he pleased and encouraged others to do the same.

"Once the rebellion was discovered God sent his archangel, Michael, to throw Lucifer and his followers out of heaven and protect heaven from any further rebellion. Michael threw them into hell and earth where they ruled until a redeemer was sent to resurrect them to their former state."

"Lucifer, realizing what he had done, repented and sought to make amends for his deeds. A penance was decided upon by God and the other angels in heaven. Lucifer must subordinate his will to the will of God until he preferred God's will to his own, and he must help those angels he encouraged to rebel by showing them his preference for God's will over his own. If this were done, the Morning Star would shine again in the heavens."

In this legend we have the whole story of the companions' struggle with free will and independent consciousness, even though it is difficult to consider the lost companions as being symbolized by Lucifer and his fellow angels! But according to the secret teachings, they are the fallen angels, lost to their original purpose and nature through their own use of free will and independent consciousness. But, even Lucifer is a creation of God, and God wishes that not one of His creations is lost. So a way was prepared for all to return to their former place.

Beyond weaving the story of the companions through the fabric of life there were other important things that had to be done if the rescue was to be accomplished. One of these was the preparation and perfection of the physical body.

THE PHYSICAL BODY

Entering into the influences of the earth was not a quick, single transition from spirit to form, from universal consciousness to physical consciousness, but a long descent through many levels of consciousness down eventually to a level with only three dimensions and the duality of opposites. By the time the companions came close to the influences of the earth they were already far from their original consciousness and nature.

In order for them to experience this realm a three-dimensional form was needed, but no forms were available for the wayward companions because they were never meant to manifest in this realm. Nevertheless, they were determined to do so, and began to use whatever forms were available. In some cases they adapted the available forms to better suit themselves, but none were human bodies like we know them today. Only the plant, animal and mineral kingdoms were on the earth when the companions began to enter; many of the first ones to arrive used these forms to manifest into and experience three-dimensional

35

life. The strange creatures that remain in our legends today were the results of this forceful entry into the early earth: satyrs (beings that were half goat and half man), centaurs (half horse and half man), dryads (women living in trees, and often an entire "enchanted" forest of them), sphinxes (half man and half lion, ram or hawk; also a winged lion with a woman's head and breasts), and the mermaids and mermen.

The souls that did not immediately force their way in could see that this was not good and they would have to perfect a body just for the companions to use. In this way the companions could manifest in a form more reflective of their true nature. It was also a law of nature that all creatures should give life only to their own kind.

The rescuing souls began influencing the evolutionary cycles of the earth forms until they could breed a form that closely approximated what they needed. The next step required the help of the creator. In order for the form to be precisely for the companions it needed to be enlivened by the original creator of life. The companions had the power to create. They were truly co-creators with God, and they had created many things, some beautiful, some ugly. But the final

36

form for manifesting in the earth needed that special spark of life that only the creator could give. The Creator knew the needs of its lost companions and their hearts; so it added the final touch to the new physical form on the earth, the human body, and the companions began to live on the earth. Once the human body was perfected all those with strange bodies were corrected, until the companions were inhabiting only human bodies.

The perfected bodies were then separated into two forms, a male and a female form. As I explained earlier, the companions were by nature androgenous, male and female in one, but in order for them to manifest in the realm of duality and form it was necessary to divide these two aspects of the soul. Therefore, only one aspect of an incarnate soul is dominantly manifesting, usually it is reflected by the sex of the physical body being used, but not always. A soul could be manifesting its female aspect and yet incarnate in a male body, and vice versa. There are many reasons for separating these two aspects of the soul while it incarnates, the chief one being of all things, loneliness. Togetherness in the celestial realm was natural, but the third dimension required clear demarcations of space and time. The souls were alone inside separate bodies, and not only was it more difficult to companion with fellow souls, but because of the loss of contact with the creator, one felt totally on one's own, without connection to anything but oneself. Therefore it was deemed best to separate the female and male aspects and create a relationship where two souls could reunite on the earth and give some sense of wholeness and togetherness to earth life. It also provided a physically natural way to reproduce the bodies according to the laws of nature. This would become very important as the companions continued to lose more and more of their awareness of their spiritual selves, eventually becoming totally physical in consciousness. At this stage of incarnating they would be totally subject to the laws of nature and without any of their supernatural powers.

In the first chapters of Genesis we find a very similar description of the early periods on the earth. Let me retell key parts of the Biblical Genesis and add the interpretations from the Secret Teachings:

Genesis 1:26—"And God said, Let us make man in our image, after our likeness: and let them have dominion over the fish of the sea, and over the fowl of the air, and over the cattle, and over all the earth, and over every creeping thing that creepeth upon the earth."

Interpretation: God's companions are created in God's image, they are like God, and they are given power to do as they please with all of the creation.

Genesis 1:27—"So God created man in his own image, in the image of God created he him; male and female created he them."

Interpretation: Each man is like God, having both the female and male aspects within themselves. This is the spiritual creation of "man" or the souls. They are at this point only spiritual. The earth is still without form but the idea of the earth and its creatures has been created.

Genesis 2:4, 5 & 6—"These are the generations of the heavens and the earth when they were created, in the day that the Lord God made the earth and the heavens, And every plant of the field *before it was in the earth,* and every herb of the field *before it grew:* for the Lord God had not caused it to rain upon the earth, and *there was not a man to till the ground.*"

All of this is written *after* the seven days of

creation had ended. Two creations were being described, the first occurred in the spirit and the second occurred in the physical.

It is only after God created man in His image (1:27) that the Lord God creates a physical form for man to enter and live in while on the earth physically—

Genesis 2:7—"And the Lord God formed man of the dust of the ground, and breathed into his nostrils the breath of life; and man became a living soul."

According to the secret teachings this is the creation of the body for manifesting in the earth. But, it was the will of the soul that caused this to be done, not God's will. God had already finished the "seven days" of creation. Yet, since the souls had forced themselves into the physical it was necessary for them to have bodies of their own, not animal or plant bodies.

However, even after this new body was completed the souls were still not thriving. The nature of physical life was such that they were lonely.

Genesis 2:18—"And the Lord God said, It is not good that the man be alone; I will make him an help meet for him. (verse 22) And (from) the rib, which the Lord God had taken from man, made he woman, and brought her unto the man."

Interpretation: From out of the androgenous man, the Lord God separated the female aspect and gave it separate form.

The body that was eventually developed for the companions is like our body as it is today. It is a miniature copy of the universe, possessing physical, mental and spiritual forces. These forces are so closely blended together that the impressions of one have an affect on the other two: what one eats can affect one's thinking and thinking can affect digestion, spiritual inspiration can effect physical conditions and so on. This is the vehicle of God's companions while they abide in the material plane and, as such, it is the temple of the "living God."

Within this body are seven spiritual centers through which the soul manifests in the three-dimensional world. These centers or chakras correspond with the endocrine glands and certain plexus along the cerebrospinal system. Through these channels the forces of the spiritual live in three-dimensional form, and through these centers the incarnate soul can attune to its spiritual self and its God.

41

These seven centers also correspond to the seven colors of the spectrum that appear when a beam of white light is refracted. Here again the symbology is subtly beautiful: the central, whole being is like a beam of white light and as it passes through physical dimensions, represented by the prism, only its parts are seen.

The centers also correspond to the seven notes of the musical scale, and to seven of the major planets in our solar system as indicated in the following diagram. Not surprisingly, they also correspond to the seven dwarfs in Snow White who work deep in the mines and have a very sloppy house before Snow White comes and straightens it out for them. The four lower centers correspond to the four elements of the earth plane: earth, wind, water and fire. In fact, the four lower centers correspond to the earth while the three higher centers are heaven.

The body of the companions is a reflection of their cosmic, universal selves, and as such it is a temporary terrestrial home for these celestial beings.

SPIRITUAL CENTERS OF THE BODY

NUMBER	GLANDS	CORRESPOND TO	EASTERN CHAKRA	PLEXUS
6	PINEAL	MIND & KNOWING MERCURY INDIGO "la"	CROWN CHAKRA	BRAIN PLEXUS
7	PITUITARY	STRENGTH & SPIRITUALITY JUPITER VIOLET "ti"	THIRD EYE CHAKRA	
5	THYROID PARATHYROID	PSYCHIC & WILL POWER URANUS BLUE "so"	THROAT CHAKRA	CERVIC PLEXUS
4	THYMUS	LOVE & RIGHT ACTIONS & THOUGHTS VENUS GREEN "fa" AIR	HEART CHAKRA	CARDIAC PLEXUS
3	ADRENALS PANCREAS SPLEEN, ETC.	MADNESS & FORGIVENESS MARS YELLOW "mi" FIRE	NAVEL CHAKRA	SOLAR PLEXUS
2	CELLS OF LEYDIG	MYSTIC & GUIDANCE NEPTUNE ORANGE "re" WATER	LOWER ABDOMEN CHAKRA	
1	OVARIES OR TESTES	FLESH & BODILY NEEDS SATURN RED "do" EARTH	ROOT OR KUNDALINI CHAKRA	PELVIC PLEXUS

ORIGINAL SIN

Before we leave Genesis let's look at how man and woman originally sinned. From the Secret Teachings we know they were actually celestial beings who became terrestrial by their own doing and thought of themselves as little more than bodies. Furthermore, being in the physical plane was *not* their ultimate purpose for existence. It was hoped they would come to know and love God enough to seek His companionship *in the spirit*, not in the flesh. With all of this in mind let's review the Genesis story of original sin.

The earthbound souls, now represented by Adam and Eve, were forbidden to eat the fruit from "The Tree of the Knowledge of Good and Evil," because if they did, as the serpent well knew (3:4 & 5), they would know they were really gods within God and had free will to do whatever they pleased. The serpent neglected to tell them that they had already used their free will to force their way into the earth, an act they would not be proud of if they knew the difference between good and evil—especially if they became aware of it before they were ready to face God with such knowledge. If they ate the fruit before

43

they were ready, their shame and guilt would so overwhelm them that they would not want to be near God's all-seeing consciousness. By restricting their awareness of good and evil it gave them time to live in God's manifested presence and gradually regain an awareness of their true nature and purpose, all in the protection represented by the garden. But once again they chose to do what they wanted, and they ate the fruit! The resulting knowledge caused them to feel immense guilt, so much so that they hid from God, feeling they were "naked." The awareness of good and evil and the subsequent guilt made God's efforts to help them even more difficult. Now they were going to have to go even farther away from God's presence until they could feel redeemed enough to seek His presence again.

The author of Genesis subtly reveals this growing distance from God by changing the name of God as the companions continued to move farther away. First, man was created by "God," then when he entered the physical world his body was made by the "Lord God" with whom he shared the garden. Finally, after the loss of the garden he could only relate to the divine as,

"Lord."

For a long time things got progressively worse. Cain and Abel could only relate to their creator through altar sacrifices. Eventually the people could not even conduct their own altar sacrifices; it had to be done for them by an anointed one, a priest, prophet or holy man. Still later they wanted one of their members to be appointed king over them so he could tell them what to do. Their personal, direct relationship with the creator was becoming blocked by layers of protective barriers, until the people no longer knew they were meant to be personal companions to the creator. In fact, this was the principal crime that led to Jesus' being sentenced to death: He claimed to be the Son of God, in personal touch with God, and God was his father. This claim was too much for the authorities to accept; no man was that closely related to God. This shows just how far away from their true natures man had come.

Let's return to the garden again. Since the souls had come to know what they had done and who they were by eating the forbidden fruit, it was imperative that their hiding from the creator not go on forever. After all they were supposed to

eventually become the companions of the creator.
And so, the fruit from The Tree of Life (represen-
ting unlimited access to the spirit, which is the life
force and therefore, immortality) was taken away
from them and protected from them. They would
no longer have unlimited access to life's "power
source" as they had always had before this fall.
Now they would have only as much life or spirit
as they *sought* through attunement to the spirit
while incarnate. The less they remained attuned
to their true life source, the more they had to con-
sume what little of the elan vital they had. When
it ran out, they could no longer sustain the body
and it would die, leaving them without a physical
vehicle in which to manifest. In this way they
would not be able to make a permanent home in
the third dimension as terrestrial beings and
would be forced to experience and refamiliarize
themselves with the other dimensions from
which they had originally come.

THE PASSAGE THROUGH THE REALM

Now the pattern for the soul involved in the
earth was set. It would sojourn in the third dimension in a human body living in time and

46

space, physical form and duality. The realm would be "The Land of Choice," where each soul would be presented with those choices that would lead to the fulfillment of self and self's desires or those that would lead to the fulfillment of one's purpose with the Divine. Hopefully the soul would apply itself to the positive choices that presented themselves in this unique realm, selecting good over evil, truth over falsehood, others' needs over self's wants, the harmony of the Whole over the pleasures of selfishness; and hopefully the companion would reach beyond self and seek again a conscious awareness of the creator. All of this would require subduing the incompatible drives of one's free will and getting control over the forces and illusions of the physical world. Furthermore, the soul would have to meet the consequences of its actions; healing the wounds it inflicted on itself and others, righting the wrongs, and untying the fetters it placed on itself and others.

By making the right choices and living more and more like a companion of the creator the soul could regain its previous consciousness and state. But it was a tremendously difficult task, requiring a very long time as the earth counts time. Many

47

cycles of being in-the-body making choices and resolving previous actions, then being in-the-spirit working with the many aspects of the growing soul and consciousness would be needed before the change could be complete.

With each physical life came the opportunity to not only desire the former state of spirit consciousness and companionship with the creator, but to actually *live it* through actions, thoughts and choosing the eternal over the temporary, harmony over discord, cooperation over rebellion, the Universal over self. The more one chose the fruits of the spirit, the more one became the spirit again, freeing oneself of the possessive powers of the physical. Eventually this would lead to a new awareness of actually *being* a spirit, a soul *in* a body rather than thinking one was only a body.

With each death in the physical came the birth again into the spirit body and the opportunity to reflect on how well the individual used the opportunities available in its most recent incarnation. The memories and impressions left from the souls' incarnation gave it strength and encouragement for completing the task of the reunion of its original consciousness and pur-

PATH OF REINCARNATION

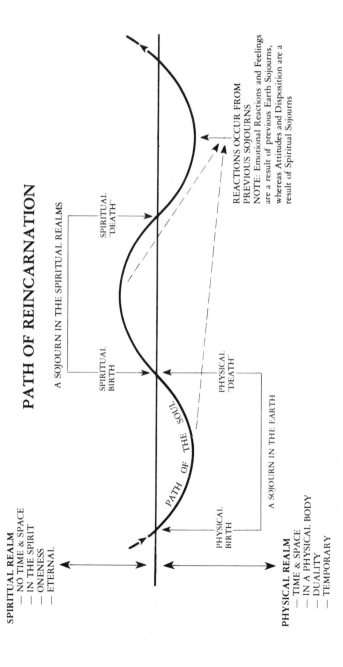

A SOJOURN IN THE SPIRITUAL REALMS

SPIRITUAL "DEATH"

SPIRITUAL BIRTH

PHYSICAL "DEATH"

PATH OF THE SOUL

PHYSICAL BIRTH

A SOJOURN IN THE EARTH

SPIRITUAL REALM
— NO TIME & SPACE
— IN THE SPIRIT
— ONENESS
— ETERNAL

PHYSICAL REALM
— TIME & SPACE
— IN A PHYSICAL BODY
— DUALITY
— TEMPORARY

REACTIONS OCCUR FROM
PREVIOUS SOJOURNS
NOTE: Emotional Reactions and Feelings
are a result of previous Earth Sojourns,
whereas Attitudes and Disposition are a
result of Spiritual Sojourns

pose. As one proved to itself, others and the creator that it not only desired the former state but actually lived it and chose it, then one gained strength over its guilt and doubt, and came again into the presence of God, its father and companion. In the spirit body between sojourns in the earth, the companion worked in other realms akin to this one.

All aspects of consciousness and life must be experienced and perfected as the soul grows toward its ultimate purpose.

Now that the passage through the difficult physical dimension was set and the way to the creator clear, there remained only for some soul to go through it and reach the other side. By doing so this soul would show the way and make it easier for others to get through. But who would be first? Most of the lost ones were so busy with their own pursuits that they didn't even care about the passage; but many longed to return home and regain their true place, yet they were doubtful, weak and weary of the effort required. According to the secret teachings, the first soul to volunteer to go through every trial, overcome every temptation, dispel every illusion, conquer every challenge and reach perfection was that soul we call Jesus of Nazareth.

THE FIRST BEGOTTEN SON

"No man has ascended up
to heaven but he that came
down from heaven, even the
Son of man. . ."
—Jesus Christ (John 3:13)

The soul who eventually became known as Jesus was the first to pass through the perils and pitfalls latent in the gifts of free will and independent consciousness. Passing through it all he reached Oneness with the Father, the Creator, becoming the First Begotten of the Father.

According to the Secret Teachings, this soul passed through all the various stages of development and by complying with the Universal Law it perfected each stage until its will, its desire, its mind, its soul was one with the creator's, thus fulfilling the purpose for which it was created and showing the way to all others who would choose to follow. By doing this, Jesus became the model, the way, the example for all the souls in and around the influences of the earth.

He entered the difficult, blinding world of form and lived through every phase of it, overcoming it and regaining his former state of consciousness. He perfected the forces of the mind, of power, of flesh, of love, of death, of the soul and of consciousness. Being perfect in all things, he instructed others to do the same (Matt. 5:48).

He did not accomplish all of this in one physical lifetime as we are commonly led to believe, nor was he born perfect as some insist. He was born a man like all men but he had assumed a purpose and a mission that made him very different from most men: He was to live like a man, experience the same temptations as all men, the same challenges, the same weaknesses, but through compliance with the law and the Father's will he would overcome each. It was not accomplished quickly or easily. He suffered; he experienced losses, broken hearts, deaths, and confusion. It took him thirty sojourns in the earth to accomplish all that the creator gave him to do; the last of these sojourns was as Jesus of Nazareth, the Anointed One, the Christ. This is not to say that this soul has not been on the earth since that life, quite the contrary. According to many sources,

51

he continues to enter and help with the continuing rescue of the other companions. But, let's look at some of his incarnations as he perfected the way.

His first appearance, as Paul indicates (1 Cor. 15:45), was as Adam in which he became a living soul and first experienced the loss of God's presence and the pain of death. Then he came again as Enoch who walked and talked with God and left the earth without dying (Gen. 5:24). In Adam he was not born but was created by God, yet through original sin he came to know death. As Enoch he was born into the flesh but did not experience death.

He appeared again as the High Priest Melchizedek, who was neither born nor died.

Next he came as one of the sons of Jacob, subjected to all the influences of men and their goings-on, but holding fast to that faith that the heavenly Father would be near even in the most desolate places. In this incarnation he was called Joseph. He was sold by his brothers and taken into the land of the Pharaoh, alone and imprisoned, yet knowing the Father was always aware of him and that the opportunity would come for him to rise to a position of great power and influence, and be a blessing to his brothers who had sold him away. This life was a major one in preparation for his entry as Jesus the Savior in which he would manifest his oneness with God and the true nature of all men as spirits and gods, not bodies or terrestrial beings.

Then, he became involved in the activities of the earth as Joshua. In this experience he learned to partake of the earth, yet become less and less earthly-minded.

Even as Jesus he faced tests, first with the three temptations of the devil and then in the garden where he struggled with his personal desire not to experience the final test and God's desire that he do so. The last for him to overcome was death of the body and submission of his will to the will of the Father. In passing through these he gained power over death and complete oneness with the Father. To truly comprehend what this accomplishment was we need to realize that his body was drained of all its natural fluids, blood and water, and was completely dead for three days—but it came to life again. According to Jesus' own teachings, it is the spirit that gives life, not the flesh. The absence of spirit is physical death and the presence of spirit gives life again,

even to a three-day-old dead body. Lazarus' body
was dead for a week and Jesus called Lazarus to
enter it again. For those souls who have come
to believe only in the reality of this terrestrial
world these are impossible feats. Once one
realizes that he is a spirit and the spirit lives
continuously, then raising the empty three-
dimensional vehicle with the spirit is easy. However, having knowledge of something and having
the power that comes from true understanding
of it are two different things. We can hear something and even believe in it, but we will rarely act
as though we believe it unless we have personally
experienced it.

Saying we are the children of God and the
eventual companions of God who have gone
astray for a time, and we are actually celestial
beings of spirit, mind and soul with free will and
independent consciousness is all very easy, but
really believing it and *being* it is entirely a different matter. In the experiences of the soul Jesus
we can see how all phases of the fall from grace,
the struggle with the distracting forces of self's
will, the influences of the physical and the rise
again to the original consciousness can be
achieved—slowly, patiently, step by step, line

upon line, here a little there a little and before you know it you are there. This is not thinking or believing you are a celestial being, companion of the creator, but actually *being* it.

These ideas and promises found in the teachings of Jesus and the secret teachings about Jesus are not idle, casual things said to inspire or comfort anyone, they are as real as breathing. Neither are they something from long ago, without relevance to life today. For in Jesus was and is the pattern for us to regain our sense of divinity, of spirituality while in a material world. His passage opens the door for us from the physical world into the light and understanding of the spiritual. We, too, must pass from life to "death" and life again. We must pass through all the tests, even as He, until we are perfect, even as our eternal companion is perfect.

THE LAND OF CHOICE

Hundreds of thousands of years have now passed since the companions first entered the earth. In some ways it must seem as though the rescue has failed. As we look around the planet we still see hundreds of millions of souls who seem to have little awareness of their true nature, their true purpose for living. We see injustice, cruelty, war, violence, all kinds of suffering and deprivation. Yet, in the midst of all of this the rescue continues—quietly, little by little, soul by soul. It's as though there were two worlds here on earth, one focused on the day-to-day activities of this physical planet, with its nations, cities, businesses, races, languages, religions, schools and endless activities, and another focused on the universal, timeless growth of the souls and their relationship with and awareness of the First Cause, the Creator, the Universal Consciousness. Amid the buying and selling, the building up and tearing down, the fighting and the loving is a gentle rising awareness of the brotherhood of all the peoples on the planet and a sense of the spirit that survives the material.

There still remains the tendency to seek for solutions among the things of this world when it can only be found *within* the inner place of one's being. It is not outside among the many physical manifestations of this world, but within the consciousness, soul, mind and spirit of each individual. The physical world is not to be ignored; in fact, it plays a major part in the soul's reunion as we will see.

Chapter Four

DESTINY, FATE & KARMA

Every thought, every action, every idle word sets up *re*actions according to the Universal Law. These reactions become the fate, the destiny and the karma of the soul. The soul is destined by the law to meet its own thoughts, words and actions face to face. It truly does make the bed it will lie in, plant the field it will harvest and experience the effects of its own causes. This is not punishment or retribution, but merely an impersonal law of the universe. Independent consciousness and free will are gifts. However, each gift comes with complete responsibility for its use. Every free-willed action will bring upon the soul a similar reaction. The law is perfect, simple and clear. In fact, every good action brings good upon the doer, too.

An individual's fate is simply the result of previous choices made by the individual. The reason the effects of these previous choices often seem unjustified is because our horizon is too limited. We do not see the whole picture. We look no further then a person's birth for causes, not realizing that he or she is actually a continuously living soul with eons of experiences prior to its most recent physical birth.

"Master, who did sin, this man, or his parents, that he was born blind?" (John 9:1 & 2.) Now if these disciples didn't believe in and understand reincarnation and karma, why would they ask if this man's own sins had caused him to be *born* blind? The only way this could happen is for him to have sinned *before* his birth! And, in fact, that is just what they thought he might have done. Notice also how the disciples thought that his parents' sins might have caused the condition. In this case, they would be meeting their sin in having a blind child.

The companions of God are free to live and choose and grow as they desire, but not without being subject to universal spiritual laws. Through meeting one's thoughts, actions and words one learns to discern wisdom from folly, lasting strength from weakness and true life from illusionary ego trips. The law is actually a magnificent tool for perfect learning. It is completely impersonal, everyone experiences it equally, as indicated in this verse from Hebrews (5:8), "Though he were a Son, yet learned he obedience by the things which he suffered."

This law is not some fierce god in the sky keeping track of everything people do so it can zap them when they least expect it. Most karmic reactions come from the individual's own deep memory of what it has done with its freedom, and as the individual comes closer to fulfilling its purpose of being a companion with the creator it becomes uncomfortable with the incompatible memory, so it seeks to resolve it. A typical example would go something like this: Suppose a soul wrongfully criticizes another soul among his peers and behind his back. As he becomes more aware of his true nature he will recall this wrong and because of its incompatibility with the creator, he will seek to correct it. Now, the resolution could take many forms. He could be found working closely with the injured soul as a supporter, assistant, publicist, agent and so on. Or perhaps he'd find himself in a position to wrongfully criticize the other person again, and to the same peers. Then the test would be to see if he chooses not to, even if it means a certain loss of position to himself. Throughout all of this the soul grows wiser and more sensitive to spirit and its ways.

If, however, a soul has gotten so far away from its true nature that it has no conscience, then the law can become a formidable obstacle to any further free-will actions by that soul. The soul simply is surrounded by its karma; everywhere it turns it meets the terrible effects of its previous actions. Yet, even a soul who has gotten in this pathetic situation can return to perfection through patiently meeting every bit of its karma, because there is no total condemnation from the creator or the law. If the soul turns away from its selfish incompatible ways and begins acting, thinking and speaking like a Son or Daughter of God, then the law is just as perfect as it is with error; and the *re*actions begin to build and establish a new destiny for the soul.

The law also works in some very curious ways. One of the most paradoxical has to do with God's desire that no soul is lost forever. Because of this divine desire there is a quirk in the law that somehow causes one's greatest weakness to become its greatest potential strength. With each difficult situation, whether it is a physical, mental or spiritual one, there comes an opportunity. These "opportunities" sometimes appear to be hopeless problems, like a crippling disease, an uncontrollable habit or a situation in which one feels totally victimized without cause. More often they are seen as mere annoyances or frustrations, like an unattractive nose, a difficult sibling, spouse, colleague, boss, lover or friend, or the ever present lack of money. In all these cases, the soul has an opportunity to resolve and overcome some weakness in itself, and by doing so with the right attitude the soul can rise to new heights of consciousness, love and companionship. Attempting to sidestep one's crosses is simply a temporary diversion, delaying the eventual glorification that is the soul's inheritance when it seeks it.

All has to be met. And yet, no soul is given more than it can bare to carry—this is the paradoxical blessing in the limitations of time and space. A soul is given the time it needs to turn away from its selfish ways, and like the prodigal son return home to a feast of joy and welcome from its father in heaven. Reincarnation is not a way to avoid judgment and responsibility, it is a way to allow the soul enough time to correct its mistakes and develop itself.

Associated with these "quirks" in the law is the most amazing aspect of the law, grace. Grace is like getting a temporary release from the law in order to get oneself back together. When a soul turns around from its self-oriented ways and begins to look again for its original purpose and first love, the law is temporarily suspended. This gives the seeking soul time to gather its strength for the journey home. The soul will still have to meet itself and its thoughts, actions and words along the way, but it will be up to the task because of grace.

THE DYNAMICS OF FATE

As an illustration, suppose while travelling on a road you arrive at a point where the road divides into two and you must decide which road you will take. Once you make your decision you have set a direction that can be almost totally predicted. In this way your fate is decided, but remember it was your free decision that cast it in the first place. Now suppose that we could fly up in the air and get a bird's eye view of the road you have selected to travel. From this vantage point we would see your future. The catch is that we couldn't be absolutely sure you'd stay on this road once you started. You may decide to go back to the beginning of the road and take the other one, or you may choose to take a sideroad off of this road, or you may even decide to sit down for a long time in one place along this road. In this way, your fate is before you, but you still have the free will to change your direction. It may take you some time before you can make a significant change and perhaps it will require some considerable effort. For example, let's suppose you did decide you wanted to travel a different road. Where you are on the present road will in some way determine what options are available to you. There may only be one side road within miles of you. You might be close enough to the beginning of the road to turn around, or too far down the road for that, in which case you'd have to push on until you could choose another route. Many of the decisions in our lives are like this. They are affected by our original choices, which may be long forgotten by now. They are also affected by the nature of the road we're on, thus our options are affected by our location. Nevertheless, no matter where we are in our life, no matter what circumstances we find ourselves in, when we finally wake up and take notice of what we're doing, there remains our free will to make the necessary changes. The only limitation is how long it will take us to get to the place where we can make a significantly new choice and how much effort will be required to get there.

"IT'S MY KARMA"

One of the most distorted views of karma is the idea that we can't do anything about it. No matter how terrible our predicament, there is always something we can do, even if it is just to deal with it as best we can, with a patient smile, a good attitude and a loving heart. The time will come when we will be through with this stretch of the hard road, and it's best to come out of it with no bitterness. No one has done this to you, it is a result of your own actions, thoughts or words. In patience you will overcome it and rise again to an even greater level than before. Remember that in the worst situation lies the greatest opportunity.

THE CENTER IN THE
MIDST OF CONDITIONS

From *The Secret of the Golden Flower* we find another beautiful concept: Amid all the circumstances of our life, all its activities, all its demands, there lies deep within us an undisturbed, unmoved place of ultimate quiet and peace. This is the center in the midst of conditions. When we learn how to enter this place for short periods each day, the demands of the day lose much of their sting. We can not only cope better, but we will actually make better decisions and effect better use of our time and energy each day. Later, in the section on Meditation we'll discover some of the techniques for entering this special place.

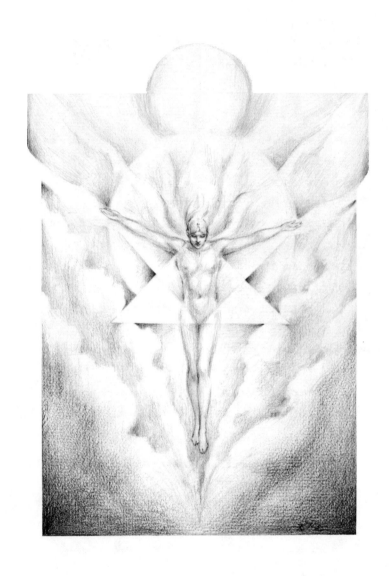

PART TWO

HOW TO FULFILL YOUR ULTIMATE PURPOSE

Chapter Five

THE TOOLS OF
THE AWAKENING

Fortunately there are some very practical tools for achieving the reawakening of our inner-selves and attuning to the Universal Consciousness. These are tools that anybody can learn to use skillfully, achieving significant results. At first they may not appear like very powerful or effective tools for such a grand endeavor, but after one uses them for a while their effectiveness becomes profoundly evident. Some of the tools are very ancient, going back to the earliest days on earth; and they have been refined into precision instruments by many dedicated souls along the way. Some of them originated in the eastern areas of this world, Tibet, India, China and Japan. Others have their roots in the western hemispheres. But, all of them have one common purpose behind them, to help regain that consciousness that was lost when we entered this dimension in pursuit of our own desires.

I have personally worked long and hard with each of these tools, and I've listened to many others who have worked with them longer than I have. Their power is subtle, requiring persistance and patience, but amazingly effective and true. Nevertheless, the proof is in the tasting. Try them for yourself, and don't hesitate to modify them to suit your preferences. But, do give them a sincere try and enough time to reward you with their hidden treasures.

THE POWER OF AN IDEAL

All of us, whether consciously or unconsciously, live by some standard of excellence, some image of what a man or woman is, and we measure ourselves against that image or standard. In some cases, we only see this image in the fragmented form of roles—a man is different when he is in the role of father than he would be in the role of soldier.

The image we hold in our inner mind affects our perceptions of ourselves and others.

It also is the motivation behind most of our actions, thoughts and words.

The standard by which we measure ourselves is usually determined by our childhood models, our culture and many social, racial, religious, and economical factors. Even the state of our health and the appearance of our body affect the image we hold as excellent. In addition to these more commonly accepted factors, we are also bringing with us very deep soul memories from experiences prior to this incarnation. In many cases, these also shape our inner image or ideal. Then, we tend, whether consciously or unconsciously, to evaluate ourselves and our life by how well we measure up to the image we see as excellent.

The standard, the image or the ideal has a very powerful influence on us and those around us, but most of us allow the ideal to be shaped only by those factors just mentioned. The greatest step we can take to regain our divinity and true consciousness is to decide for ourselves what our ideal will be. Next, we need to describe the ideal in as clear an image as we can, developing it on three levels, Spiritual, Mental and Physical. What is the standard of excellence by which we will measure our progress physically through our daily actions and words, mentally through our thoughts and attitudes, and spiritually through our overriding consciousness, purpose and motivation? For the standard to have its greatest power it must be the highest possible image we can conceive as perfect, something that we can always strive for and may one day achieve. If we set an ideal like this and each day work at moving closer and closer to actually being that ideal, it will launch us into a whole new level of growth and expansion of consciousness.

In practice, the ideal or standard is not a static image, but is forever expanding as we grow closer to it. The nearer we come to reaching our standard the more we see an even greater standard beyond it. It is an ever expanding vision of the breadth of life, consciousness and being. Just imagine for a minute that you really are a lost companion of the creator of this entire universe, not just the universe we see with our eyes, but all the unseen dimensions of it as well! Only then is it easy to see how your ideal today will not be near sufficient for you tomorrow. Eventually, the standard you measure yourself by will be that of your Divine Companion and you will strive to be perfect even as He is. Perfection certainly appears to be a very ambitious goal as we view ourselves today.

There's an important, subtle characteristic to this technique of setting and living by an ideal. It is not so much the "what" of your ideal as it is the "why" of it. Why you are setting and living by an ideal is going to determine more about your companionability with the divine than the details of your ideal. One must search one's heart often to make sure that self-glorification, self-gratification, self-aggrandizement, self-centeredness, self-willfulness and just plain self is not the reason you seek fulfillment. If the path we are on makes us more humble, more meek, more patient, then it is the right path and it will lead to the ultimate fulfillment of knowing oneself to be oneself and yet one with the Whole.

Another critical aspect of setting and living by an ideal is an awareness that the true aspect of real life, flows *from* out of the spirit into the mental where it takes on a clearer image and then manifests itself in the physical world. Therefore, the ideal must originate with the spiritual impetus if it is to bring that metamorphic

71

change from material consciousness to spiritual or Christ consciousness, terrestrial nature to celestial nature, from "son of man" to "Son of God" (and Daughter, too).

Let the image, the standard, the ideal come from your higher self, then take hold of it and shape your mental and physical ideals around it. In this way you will really begin the process with the right direction.

Very practically speaking, you should begin developing your new ideal by praying, meditating, holding your thoughts on the things of the spirit, and watching your dreams. After you think you have a "feel" or sense of what your higher self seeks in the way of a spiritual ideal, then sit down and write this spiritual standard by which you are going to live. Then let this shape your mental ideal—how are you going to think and what is going to be your attitude toward yourself, your life and the others in your life? Now let this help shape your physical ideal—how are you going to act, especially what are you going to do in your daily life with the daily situations. This again should be related to yourself, your life and the others in your life.

Each day you should review these ideals

and reflect on how well you're doing. Try reflecting on this while in touch with your higher self, you'll gain better insight this way. If you feel your ideal is changing, then make the change in writing and begin to live accordingly. Before you know it, people will be telling you how much you've changed, and you'll know it, too. It is a wonderful experience, the value of which can only be appreciated through directly experiencing it firsthand.

DAILY APPLICATION

There are two old sayings that go something like this, "There is no surer way of getting where you want to go than to keep on keeping on," and the other goes like this, "The journey of a thousand miles begins with one step—and continues step by step." There is a subtle, yet powerful truth in these two sayings. No matter how long or hard a journey may be, if it is taken step by step and with an unceasing determination to complete it, then it will be done. No one has to deal with the awesome thought of the whole journey, just the next step along the way.

One of the most practical ways to work with

daily application is the use of disciplines. Select one or two of your weaknesses or faults and design a daily discipline related to overcoming them. It can be as simple as trying to focus on the positive aspects of a person or task rather than the negative. Then as the opportunity arises during the day for you to see the negative, you stop yourself and refocus on the positive. Before long, you won't have to stop yourself because it will be second nature for you to focus on the positive.

The same can be done with helping others. Just select some task or attitude that another person is seeking from you and design a daily discipline whereby you do some portion of this each day. For example, your spouse may be seeking help from you with some of the mundane chores of daily life, so you decide to do the dishes every other day, or vacuum once a week.

Disciplines don't have to be awesome gestures of great character building. In fact, the greatest changes come through the little things done well and faithfully.

I can't think of an aspect of character, or work, or relationships, or any aspect of life that can't be changed by applying oneself to it daily in little ways.

MEDITATION

Developing an ability to enter into a deep meditation is a vital tool for achieving a higher state of spiritual consciousness and reuniting our separate parts.* Through meditation the quiet body, the clear, focused mind and the enlivened spirit will rise to the highest possible state of awareness that we can perceive, even into the living presence of God. Over a period of time, meditation will bring us into the awareness of our original nature and purpose, transforming us from mere mortal terrestrial beings to immortal, divine companions. It will make our present life in the earth a veritable school for soul growth. Everything will have new meaning when we are attuning ourselves daily to the highest source of life. Strength, wisdom and patience are the fruits of meditation, as are meekness and humility.

---

* BODY, MIND, SOUL AND SPIRIT, AS WELL AS CONSCIOUS. SUBCONSCIOUS AND SUPERCONSCIOUS.

BORN AGAIN AND AGAIN

No matter how far we have gotten away from our center of being, we can recontact that sacred place through daily meditation.

The right heart is the first step toward experiencing meaningful, effective meditations. The best meditation techniques won't lift a selfish heart into the presence of the Creator. We must free our minds and hearts from those things that will distract or interfere with the progress of the meditation. The right thoughts and actions, the right attitudes and emotions throughout the day will do more for our meditation than any technique.

There are many ways to meditate and as many reasons, but here we will focus our attention on those techniques that help us regain our spiritual consciousness.

Basically, meditation is quieting the physical body and conscious mind, clearing away the thoughts and cares of the day, and attuning to our inner self and there abiding in a heightened state of awareness and expectancy, quietly listening and waiting for that response from our higher self and, eventually, the Divine.

There are specific techniques and exercises for quieting the body and the mind, and arousing,

76

awakening and enlivening our spirit and soul to greater consciousness. All of these techniques use special activity to reach inactivity. Since each soul has a different perspective, a different collection of experiences and is at various levels of development, it is best that each modify the meditation techniques to suit their own comfort and preference. No one technique works for absolutely everybody, nor for two similar individuals in exactly the same way. The following meditation process is very good. It contains some of the best techniques known today and can be easily modified to suit oneself.

Begin by cleansing the body with water. Depending on the circumstances, this can be no more than splashing a little water on your face and washing your hands or it can be a shower or bath. Then sit or lie in a comfortable position. If you like, you may use one of the eastern yoga asanas (positions), but don't force yourself into a position that is going to be so unnatural or uncomfortable for you that it distracts you from achieving stillness. The ultimate goal is to still the body.

Many people find that stretching exercises before assuming the position for meditation make the body more relaxed and ready for being in one position for a long time. Another pre-meditation exercise that yields good results is to move the head forward touching the chest with the chin three times, then stretch the head backwards three times, and to each side three times, then circle the head to the left and then to the right three times.

This not only loosens up the neck and shoulder muscles but it increases the flow of blood to the head and brain.

Once you are in position, breathe in through the right nostil and exhale through the mouth three times. While you are breathing in think, "strength!" Then breathe in through the left nostril and exhale through the right three times. While you do this think of quietly awakening your inner spirit. Don't take breathing exercises too lightly. Remember how we became physical beings: "The Lord God breathed the breath of life in him and he became a living soul." Breath is life in this dimension and these exercises are using that force to raise the level of our life energy and arouse a response within us. If you can, let this air be fresh. Often the air in closed rooms is very stale, with little oxygen in it and many unwanted gases. Open a window if you can.

After you have gotten into position and completed your head and neck exercises and breathing exercises, begin to carry yourself deeper by using an incantation or soft music. Chanting "Oooommm" while feeling the sound rise from the lower spiritual centers of your body to the higher ones is a potent method of awakening the inner spiritual forces. There are many other chants that can be used with good results, but "Om" is universally recognized as touching a special cord within each of us. Another is "Aaaarrrreeeeooooommmm." In this incantation the "aaaa" sounds begin in the lower centers and as the sound changes, the energy rises through the centers to the final sound of "mmmm" at the third eye center. The secret to successful chanting is to think of it as "internal sounding." It's not external like singing. The sounds are meant to resonate inside the body, vibrating the spiritual centers into activity and awakening the inner consciousness.

At this stage in the meditation one can begin a technique called, "The Circulation of the Light." It is described in detail in the excellent book, *The Secret of the Golden Flower* (see appendix on Sources for Further Study). Basically, the circulation of the light is combining the cycle of breathing in and out with the rising and falling of the energy along the path from the lower centers to the higher, from the gonads up the spine to the pituitary body in the center of the brain system and behind the middle of the forehead. As one breathes in, the abdomen is drawn in and the energy rises upward along the spinal cord over the top of the head and down into the chambers of the seventh center. Here it meets with the universal creative forces and is transformed into "living water" (see Rev. 22:17) and as one exhales it flows down along the front of the body, bathing the centers as it goes. The cycle is continued until there is felt a definite raising of the vibrations of the body.

During the circulation of the light along this path and in the centers, the body may become conscious of distinct vibrations. This is different with each individual, but there are some common sensations that occur. A sensation of energy moving from the lower parts of the body upward to the head is common. This can even result in a feeling that the body is moving back and forth, side to side or in a circular motion. It can culminate at the head or reach to areas slightly above the head, like the flame over the disciples' heads when the Holy Spirit descended upon them. There may also be a feeling of lightness, slight dizziness and the drawing back of the head slightly. Within the spiritual centers one may feel vibrations, "pressures" or sensations. These are indications of the awakening of the spiritual forces. After the circulation of the light has been through enough cycles to arouse one to a higher vibrational rate, like changing water to steam, then the consciousness should move its attention away from the breathing and let it go on its own again. When the thoughts are quiet and the body is still, one should bring forth the highest Ideal it can conceive and focus on the essence of that Ideal, calling all parts of its being to rise to that Ideal. When this Ideal is in accord with that of the individual's superconscious, there will come a flow from "above" to fulfill all that is needed by the mind and the body. The individual will feel stronger, more at one with itself and the universal, and a feeling of peace and oneness will come over the individual that is rarely felt in this dimension.

I have to tell you how difficult it is to describe the deeper realms of meditation. First of all, there just aren't the words to describe it. It's as though it belongs to another dimension altogether and will never be completely describable in three-dimensional terms or concepts. Secondly, I'm not sure everyone experiences these realms in the same way. It's like asking someone if they see the same shade of a color that you are seeing—they may say yes, but do you ever really know unless you see it through their eyes? And another thing, I've never met anyone who experienced the deeper realms of meditation every time they meditated, even if they were meditating daily. So don't get too caught up in judging your meditations. Sometimes they'll be great and other times just so so. Occasionally they'll be more than you ever imagined, and you'll go in the strength of that meditation for a very long time!

It is important to remember that no matter how well one practices these techniques, if one doesn't hold fast to the right heart and mind, only harm to oneself will result. It is the pure in heart that see God (Matt. 5:8), not the skilled in meditative techniques. Here is an appropriate

82

quote from *The Secret of the Golden Flower:*

"He who lacks the right
virtue may well find
something in it, but heaven
will not grant him his Tao.*
Why not? The right virtue
belongs to the Tao* as does
one wing of a bird to the other:
if one is lacking, the other
is of no use."

Raising the spiritual forces of the body must be done for the right purpose and should be supported by daily actions and thoughts that reflect this purpose.

After meditation it is vital that one apply oneself diligently to living the Ideal throughout the daily life. It does not matter what type of work one does during a day, only that the attitude and purpose of each action supports that which the individual is seeking when it enters meditation. The person can be an innercity police officer

*THE INDIVIDUAL'S IDEAL

dealing with violence and crime all day and still be able to attune himself to his higher self and the creator if he is acting in accord with his highest Ideal.

Very few of us can begin meditating and immediately experience all the wonders of it, but if we don't start we will certainly not experience them. It is best to begin where you are and waste no time wondering why you aren't experiencing this or that. Just keep on keeping on and you are bound to experience all of it, even the voice of your creator.

It is best if you choose a specific place to meditate. This helps develop a pattern of response within the body to being in the place for meditation. Regular periods of meditation will accomplish much more than occasional periods. So, select a regular time each day and try not to miss that time. In the beginning you'll probably need only about fifteen minutes for meditation. Later you may want an hour.

Also, don't meditate on a full or hungry stomach, its bad for the digestion and makes it very difficult to achieve a deep meditation. If noises are distracting you, use the energy of those noises to raise you to a higher place of conscious-

SPIRITUAL CENTERS OF THE BODY

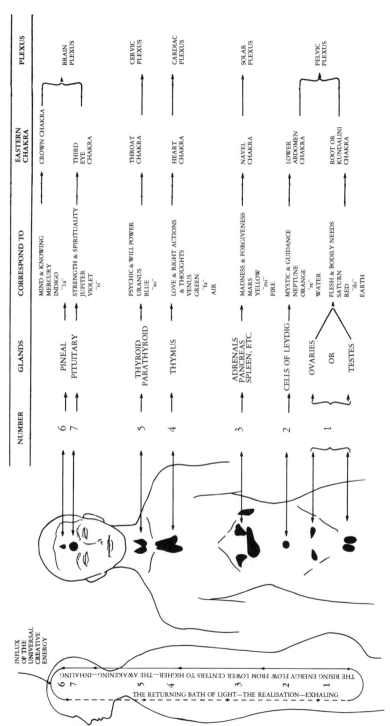

NUMBER	GLANDS	CORRESPOND TO	EASTERN CHAKRA	PLEXUS
7	PITUITARY	STRENGTH & SPIRITUALITY JUPITER VIOLET "ti"	CROWN CHAKRA	BRAIN PLEXUS
6	PINEAL	MIND & KNOWING MERCURY INDIGO "la"	THIRD EYE CHAKRA	
5	THYROID PARATHYROID	PSYCHIC & WILL POWER URANUS BLUE "so"	THROAT CHAKRA	CERVIC PLEXUS
4	THYMUS	LOVE & RIGHT ACTIONS & THOUGHTS VENUS GREEN "fa" AIR	HEART CHAKRA	CARDIAC PLEXUS
3	ADRENALS PANCREAS SPLEEN, ETC.	MADNESS & FORGIVENESS MARS YELLOW "mi" FIRE	NAVEL CHAKRA	SOLAR PLEXUS
2	CELLS OF LEYDIG	MYSTIC & GUIDANCE NEPTUNE ORANGE "re" WATER	LOWER ABDOMEN CHAKRA	
1	OVARIES OR TESTES	FLESH & BODILY NEEDS SATURN RED "do" EARTH	ROOT OR KUNDALINI CHAKRA	PELVIC PLEXUS

INFLUX OF THE UNIVERSAL CREATIVE ENERGY

THE RISING ENERGY FLOW FROM LOWER CENTERS TO HIGHER—THE AWAKENING—INHALING

THE RETURNING BATH OF LIGHT—THE REALISATION—EXHALING

ness. Don't become angry or bitter with the outside distractions. If you are caring for children, be patient and try to do the best you can to find a reasonably regular period for meditating. If you have a non-supportive spouse, don't flaunt your meditation in front of him or her; try to find a time when he or she won't be affected by your private pursuit. If you are missing the function of one of your endocrine glands because of surgery or malformation, continue to focus on the area where it would normally be and you'll get results eventually — remember the centers are spiritual first and physical second. If you find yourself falling asleep during meditation, don't be too concerned about it. Try to maintain a keen sense of quiet awareness for as long as you comfortably can, then let sleep overtake you, but only after you feel you've reached a level of heightened awareness of your Ideal.

Many people experience images, sounds, voices and other stimuli during meditation. These should be a natural response from your higher self after you have reached a keen awareness of your Ideal and not just intrusions into your meditation. So, control your consciousness in the early stages of a meditation and only relax your hold on it after you have the Ideal well in place.

SILENCE

It is easy to become so involved with the techniques of meditation that one forgets to enter into the most vital phase of meditation: silence. For many of us silence means emptiness or nothingness; to sit in silence would appear to have little value to it. However, the silence of deep meditation is anything but empty nothingness. It is remarkably revitalizing and rejuvenating, occasionally it is even filled with profound sensations, awarenesses and insights, some of which are simply indescribable but have such an impression on the individual experiencing them that he cannot forget that "feeling."

Therefore, after you have used the techniques to raise your body's vibrations and your consciousness, and aroused your soul, become as still and silent as you can. As difficult as it is to imagine, these moments in deep silence will become some of the most valuable in your life.

"And when he had opened the
seventh seal, there was
silence in heaven about the
space of half an hour."
　　　　　　—Revelations 8:1

DREAMS

In the Western world we believe knowledge is best gained through *experience* and *reasoning*. We consider intuitions, premonitions, revelations and dreams as very dubious sources for knowledge. And yet, some of our most important medical discoveries, military victories, and inventions were conceived through one of these "dubious" sources. Experience and reason are certainly valuable tools but overlooking or underestimating the value of intuitive perception, premonition, revelation and dreams is a mistake. The latter may well be more difficult to develop and more susceptible to error and to subjective interpretation, but they are well worth the effort.

Dreams are one of the best sources for insight, knowledge and understanding. When the physical body and conscious mind are quiet in sleep, the deeper levels of consciousness can more clearly express themselves. If one learns to remember these expressions and to correctly interpret them, there is no limit to one's knowledge and understanding.

I realize how difficult this is to accept given our Western training in the power and value of firsthand experience and inductive and deductive reasoning. Nevertheless, if one combined reason and experience with the power of dreams he would be able to understand anything!

At first, dreams may appear incoherent, obscure and unrelated to daily life, but with practice, one can learn the language of dreams. When studied and worked with honestly and consistently, their messages become very clear.

Nothing occurs in one's life that has not already been foreshadowed in a dream!

How can this be? Even though the predominant level of our consciousness is in the realm of time and space, the deeper levels abide in dimensions beyond time and space and can "see" the road that lies ahead. In fact, these levels of consciousness can also see the road that has been travelled, even back to the beginning of the soul's consciousness. If the conscious mind learns how to listen and understand its deeper levels of consciousness, it can know the forces affecting its life, how best to handle them and what opportunities and perils are ahead. However, the deeper consciousness is not concerned with just the profound or grand things. The everyday needs of life—money, relationships, jobs, diet, physical health, etc.—are all dealt with in dreams. Nothing is too mundane or, for that matter, too grand or holy that one cannot get insight about it from a dream.

When the conscious mind and body are asleep, the subconscious and superconscious use the images, events, people and things of daily physical life to create a somewhat three-dimensional story or message containing information that they need to convey to the conscious level. If the conscious level recalls the dream, records it, studies it, discerns its meaning and, finally, *uses* the knowledge in its life, then the whole individual begins to grow and fulfill its purposes.

Sometimes the message of a dream is very literal and clear as in this dream—

"Dreamed Betty would call tomorrow and I should not be so cool and distant. She will ask me to come visit her and I should go despite my feelings to the contrary."

Betty did call this dreamer just as the dream had predicted, and the dreamer did visit her.

Often the message of a dream has a bizarre element that helps focus the attention of the conscious mind on a particularly important part of the message, as in this dream—

"Dreamed I won my preliminary tennis match but as I went over to the stands to be congratulated by everyone my head fell off, and kept falling off. No matter what I did I couldn't keep my head on my shoulders. It was very embarrassing. Finally out of frustration I asked if anyone wanted to go watch Stan play his match. I figured if I could get them to stop looking at me I might be able to keep my head on."

By using this bizarre image the subconscious cleverly warns the conscious self of the potential for losing one's head over an initial victory and becoming too confident and perhaps losing a future match. It even gives him the solution: "Go watch your future opponent play his preliminary match."

In some cases the message of a dream is strongly stated in symbols that deeply affect the conscious self, as in this dream—

"I was in the bowels of an old, gray inner-city and on the corner was a fast-food restaurant called, 'Colonel Coffee's Coffins!' When I awoke I did not like the feeling of this dream. It was ominous and I felt like it was serious."

Apparently the dreamer's use of coffee to keep him going fast was causing serious problems within his system, perhaps literally in his bowels. This dream could be interpreted on another level as well. It could pertain to his overall lifestyle of going so fast that he would soon become like a city that had spent its wealth and was decaying.

Interpreting a heavily symbolic dream requires the dreamer of the symbols to identify what those symbols mean to him. The same symbol from two different subconsciousnesses can mean two different things. However, there are universal symbols, but even these should be applied individually. When interpreting one's dream, be careful not to prejudice your interpretation by looking for what you want to see, or by being afraid to find what you hoped for! Be as objective as you can. Pray about the dream. Sometimes it helps to set the dream aside for awhile and return to it later with a second view.

When a dream comes from the super-conscious mind, its symbolism and imagery is often like that of a vision, as in this example—

"I was aboard a large ship with twelve engines. Ten of the engines were working fine, but the eleventh engine was not assembled and the twelfth wasn't even there! I began to assemble the eleventh engine when I heard something behind me. I turned around to see a man glowing so brightly that I could hardly look at him. He started to move toward me as though he knew me, but I became extremely frightened and fell to the floor, closing my eyes and curling up into a ball as his light began to engulf me. At this moment I awoke from the dream, scared to death and sweating. The room seemed unusually dark and empty. It took me a long time to get back to sleep, even though I was praying the whole time."

Dreams from the superconscious can be very intense and filled with meaning, symbology and direct contact with everything an individual holds sacred. Without getting into too much interpretation of this dream, we can see how the dreamer's superconscious portrayed him as a ship with twelve engines (or centers) and how the conscious self was working on getting all twelve engines running properly. Because of this good work and the dreamer's seeking, he received the opportunity to actually meet the one he sought, Jesus, but it was more than he could bare at this time; certainly it prepared him for a future meeting. The dreamer told me he had only experienced the presence of Jesus once before in a dream and in that case he did not directly see him, just felt he was next to him. He was looking forward to a future meeting and hoped he wouldn't be so scared.

Here is another superconscious level dream but with a little less intensity—

"I was walking along the lake at an area where the trees hang over the bank, making it difficult to get by. As I got through the trees I was startled to see a strange man right there in front of me. At first I was very concerned, but he seemed okay. He hadn't noticed me yet. He was fishing. So I carefully continued to walk past him. As I got closer he turned and smiled. I smiled back and managed to ask if he was catching anything. He said, 'Yes, but there is one particular fish I've been trying to catch for a very long time and I just can't seem to catch her. Will you help me?' I said I would help him, and then, as though I was helping I just continued to walk by him and along the bank. After I had gotten much farther along, I realized I knew who the man was! It was Jesus. And I knew who the fish was that he wanted me to help him catch, it was me! When I woke up I felt very good, even excited and ready to go."

Not only can one meet his maker in a dream, but one can discover which stocks to buy or what school to attend and so on—just about anything from the mundane to the sublime. Here is an example of an everyday dream dealing with the practical needs of the conscious self—

"I was buying the options I had been considering and then saw myself selling puts at a profit."

This dreamer was a longtime investor in the stock market. In some cases his stock market dreams might simply be symbolic, in which case his subconscious would be using the stocks and their common terms as symbols to convey to the conscious self a message on a different topic. In this dream it seemed like an answer to his conscious mind's studies and questions about a particular option, so he bought the "puts" and a month later sold them at a profit. Very clear, simple and useful information can come through one's dreams. Here's another example—

"Dreamt my son was proud of me but he was not telling the truth. I threw the ball and he swung at it but missed, yet he said, 'Nice hit.' I said, 'Bobby, you didn't hit that ball,' but he didn't seem to care. I felt I needed to talk with him about trying to be like me or anyone else and that the truth was valuable and should not be lightly taken.

And another—

"I dreamed my lost ring was in Jim's pants pocket in the hamper."

There is literally no limit to the forms dreams can take and to the topics they can cover. Here's a dream about a previous incarnation of this soul and the effects that the occurrences of the previous life have on his present life—

"I was dressed in Spanish clothes from around the 1600's, with dark hair and a beard. I was standing in a rowboat that was slowly heading for shore. We were off the coast of what is now called St. Augustine, Florida. As we moved slowly toward shore I looked back at the ship I had just gotten off. It was surprisingly small for crossing the Atlantic Ocean; all wood and ropes and masts. On the deck I saw MaryJane (his wife in the present incarnation), but she didn't look anything like she does today. She had black hair, dark skin and dark eyes, but I knew it was MaryJane. In her arms was a child that I somehow knew was my son today (the dreamer had a three month old son in his present life). As

I watched them a strange image appeared over MaryJane's shoulder. I looked very closely and intently, trying to see what it was; then I realized it was my face as it is today! It was me, not as I was in the dream but as I look now. As I looked at this man of the future I realized that I was going to die as we reached the beach and that I would not be able to care for these two any longer, but *he* would care for them in the future. I continued to stare at his face, glancing back at MaryJane and my baby, feeling very sad that they would have to continue this life in this rough land without me to help them. Yet, as I looked back at his face I kept holding fast to the idea that he would be able to care for them in the future, and give much of the joy they were going to miss in this lifetime. Then I turned away and looked at the shoreline. It was heavily wooded and desolate. There was no sign of trouble. Then without any warning, it seemed like the beach was filled with Indians. They were wild, crazy people, yelling and screaming with a violent madness that was terrifying. Then, in slow motion, I saw the arrow heading straight for me. I felt it enter my chest, penetrating deep inside me. As I fell from the boat into the water, I turned again to the ship and

97

saw my wife and child on the deck with the face looking over their shoulders. There was no expression on their faces, and as I slowly sank in the water I continued to stare at them with all those feelings of the tragedy of the situation and what they were going to have to go through without me to help."

Not only did this dream give the dreamer an insight into one of his previous lives on the earth, but it gave him a clear view of one of his major purposes in this present life, one that he had longed for for some time—the opportunity to care for these two souls that he loved. In his present life, his wife was blond, blue-eyed and fair-skinned, but not surprisingly, she could speak Spanish, as could his present sister, even though they were all typical Anglo-Saxon Americans.

WORKING WITH YOUR DREAMS

It is easier to recall your dreams if you don't move the body right as you awake. Try to stay still with your eyes closed and gently scan your mind for any hint of the last thoughts you had before awakening. Once you get a glimpse you can usually recall more of your dream.

Pre-sleep suggestions are also helpful. As you are falling off to sleep, repeat something like the following several times: "I will sleep soundly and awake feeling refreshed, revitalized and remembering my dreams." It doesn't have to be these exact words, but you get the idea.

Keeping a dream journal and pencil beside your bed is also a very helpful tool. Your subconscious sees through the same eyes you do and when it sees you have gotten a dream journal ready, it is like a hypnotic suggestion to put something in it. The journal also gives you a great record of your dreams over a long period of time. By reading through this record you should be able to get a feel for the most common themes of your dreams which will give you a better insight into the primary concerns of your deeper consciousness or into the biggest opportunity and problem presently facing your conscious mind.

Sometimes the conscious mind is so dominant it is very difficult to get beyond its influence in dreams. When this is the case, the dream's real message is cloaked in the garments of everyday symbols that are acceptable to the conscious mind but have a deeper meaning which the conscious mind doesn't readily recognize.

This helps to present a problem that is not going to be easily accepted by the conscious self, but which, over time, must be dealt with, so the subconscious continues to raise the message behind safe images. Remember that often the conscious self is not in favor of the needs and wants of the deeper self. When the deeper self "has the floor" in sleep it must discuss the subject diplomatically if it hopes to get cooperation from the conscious self. Sometimes, however, there is no time for diplomacy and the deeper consciousness uses the most dramatic symbols it can muster to try and shake the conscious level into action. For example—

"I saw Mr. B. talking with S.L. about me. Snakes were coming out of his mouth and crawling all over the place. S.L. got very uncomfortable and backed out of the room. I knew I needed to go reassure S.L. about me before he got bit by one of the snakes. (Note: During the dream I noticed that I could walk right through the snakes without getting bitten. It was as though they knew me and weren't going to hurt me.)"

Mr. B. was a very good friend of the dreamer

so it was necessary that the deeper self use as graphic an image as possible to convey the problem Mr. B. was making behind the dreamer's back. Again the dream shows the way to resolve this problem and indicates that it is important to do it soon. Then the deeper self conveys a reassurance that the bad comments being made by Mr. B. cannot really hurt the dreamer but S.L. needed reassurance. As it turned out, S.L. was considering two people for a new position with the company and one of them was the dreamer, who after his talk with S.L., got the job.

Here is another example of a dream that tries to break through the conscious mind about a subject it does not want to discuss, adultery—

"I was sitting in the living room reading the paper when I saw a spider come under the door and walk across the room. It was very black and dangerous looking but I just didn't feel like killing it now. It went on down the hall and I thought I'd kill it later. Suddenly I heard Cindy (his wife) scream. I ran in to see what was wrong but she was just lying there on the bed as though she were dead. I shook her and called to her but nothing worked. I called the rescue squad but as soon as I touched the phone I saw red lights and sirens all around the bedroom. It was as though they already knew something was wrong and had come on their own. The chief technician looked at Cindy and then turned to me and said, 'I'm sorry, but nothing will bring her back, nothing.' Then I knew the spider that I didn't want to kill had bitten her and I would never see her again."

The dreamer woke up feeling puzzled by the dream. At first it all seemed so unrelated to his life. After all, how could a spiker kill his wife? Just in case, however, he thought he'd kill any spiders he saw in the house. It wasn't until later that he perceived another possible meaning to this dream; unfortunately, it was after Cindy had divorced him for having an affair. The dreamer said nothing could change Cindy's mind about the divorce.

Dreams are messages, lessons, discussions, guidances and warnings from our deeper levels of consciousness. If we add their influence to our lives, we will grow much more wisely.

COOPERATION

One of the most important, yet most overlooked tools of the awakening is *Cooperation*.

Fortunately for one of us God did not create

just one companion. As hard as it may be to believe, *all* of us were created in the hopes that we'd become companions to the Universal Consciousness, the Whole, or God.

This adds another dimension to our journey. Not only do we have to work on our own awakening and our personal relationship with the Creator, but we also have to learn to appreciate others and help them awaken as best we can, remembering at all times that we cannot force anyone. Each of us has free will to do as we see fit, and no one should try to get around that. But often the biggest help is not in the form of grand concepts or theories, but in simply a smile or an encouraging word.

In many instances I've seen people get along better with strangers than they do with their own close relations, such as family, friends, and colleagues. Actually, our greatest opportunities for cooperation are right in our own backyard. Each day we find ourselves face-to-face with a chance to support, encourage, comfort, love, and teach; but we often take these opportunities for granted and don't use them. It is with the very souls that we share much of our life that we can achieve much of our spiritual growth!

103

Spitefulness, backbiting, fault finding and oneupmanship are all the spirit of the anti-christ. Gentleness, comfort, encouragement, support, guidance, love, and sharing are all the spirit of the Christ Consciousness. And, it is with our closest relationships that we will find our greatest opportunities to use one of these two spirits. The more we use the fruits of the spirit, the more we become the spirit. Let's hope it's the better spirit.

An old saying that has helped me considerably when it comes to developing a spirit of co-operation is, "There is so much good in the worst of us and so much bad in the best of us that it isn't wise for any of us to think badly of the rest of us!"

Take time to work, live and participate with others and their interests. You don't want to build a heaven by yourself because once you get there you won't be very happy. Be one *with* others, yet keeping yourself on the journey you know must be travelled.

Chapter Six
CLOSING THOUGHTS

In thinking over the past fifteen years of working with the Secret Teachings and the "Tools of the Awakening" and with many different people who are doing the same, I've thought of a few things to share with you that you may find helpful in your journey.

In the beginning it is very exciting and rewarding, your whole life opens up in ways you never thought possible, but as life goes on it becomes less exciting and more a matter of doing what you know must be done. The beauty of knowing who we really are is wonderful, but living it daily can be difficult. The disciple John had a very good insight into this experience when he viewed himself eating the "book of life" during his revelation:

". . . I took the little book out
of the angel's hand, and ate
it up; and it was in my mouth
sweet as honey: and as soon
as I had eaten it, my belly was
bitter."

— Rev. 10:9

The knowledge of true life is sweet upon first tasting but, as one assimilates it, it can be bitter.

We need to keep a very special tool with us throughout the journey—*patience*. Without it I don't think any of us can make it. With patience we can continue to live in the physical world while becoming more and more alive in the spiritual one.

Keep a sense of humor, too. I've noticed that we all have a tendency to become too serious about spiritual things. Not all of physical life is evil or mundane, and not all of the resurrection is bearing a cross.

When you aren't sure about where you're going or how well you're doing, relax. Becoming uptight, worried, doubtful, skeptical or depressed is natural and to some degree, healthy;

but don't let it drag on too long. Relax. Forget about your concerns and look around for someone else to help for awhile. Become concerned about their concerns and do what you can to help them. Losing thought of yourself in helping others can do wonders for your own mental state.

When things have become too much for you, lighten the demands you're placing on yourself. Balance out your life between heavy and light, serious and funny, work and play, purposefulness and nonsense. Take a long slow walk with a child or learn a new song to sing in the shower or a new joke to share with some friends.

Another old saying that has helped me with patience and staying relaxed, yet focused on what I knew must be done is, "Be content, but never satisfied." There's a certain energy to contentment that is needed if we are to succeed without wasting ourselves, whereas satisfaction implies an acceptance of what is. We need to keep reaching beyond our present levels if we are to regain our greater state, but do so with a patient, contented energy.

Another problem along the path is the fear of evil. If we spent half as much time *seeking* the Light as we do worrying about what the darkness is up to, we'd be there by now! Certainly one should judge the forces that one is aligned with, and evil should be overcome, but all of the path is not wrestling with evil; much of it is becoming more and more familiar with Good and Light.

Don't be swayed by others or ideas of "how you're supposed to do it." Feel it out for yourself with your deeper self.

The deeper self is so naturally you that we often miss it and build an elaborate image of some angel-like figure that we don't even know and can't relate to. The deeper self sees with the same eyes, hears with the same ears and lives in the same body. It is you, and more than just you as you normally think of yourself. But, it is *you*. It's the better you.

We are spirits in bodies for a time. Our purpose for being is companionship with the Creator of the entire universe. The events we experience in our lives today are the result of our thoughts, actions and choices in the past. The sorrows, disappointments, limitations and pain we experience are opportunities to make new and wiser decisions that will change all our tomorrows.

APPENDIX

PROBLEMS WITH REINCARNATION

Here are some of the most regularly questioned aspects of reincarnation. The following excerpts are taken from the question-and-answer periods of my lectures on reincarnation.

1. If reincarnation really does occur, why don't we remember our previous lives?

Ans: The conscious mind and the subsequent personality that develops are new projections from the soul, and therefore have no memory of previous lives. If the conscious mind and personality seek within themselves, they will become aware of their soul's previous experiences. To some degree we consider the conscious mind and personality as the totality of our being, when actually they are the narrowest aspect of it. The superconscious and subconscious levels are where the memories are, and if we get in touch with these levels of ourselves we'll remember our previous lives.

2. How do you explain the population changes in the earth? Is the population increasing because new souls are entering the earth each day?

Ans: New souls are not entering the earth each day. The changes in the population of the earth are due to the entering and exiting of souls that have been involved with the earth's activities for a long, long time. Sometimes great numbers of souls leave the earth and do not return for long periods of time and when they do return, they tend to return together, causing unusual decreases and increases in the population. For example, the souls living in the ancient land of Atlantis have not been on the earth since Atlantis was destroyed. They were so highly advanced technologically that there simply wasn't anything here to interest them until the late 1800's and early 1900's. Their presence in the earth has not only helped to increase the population of the earth but it has dramatically added to the sophistication of its technology. At this time in the earth there is a strong movement of souls into manifestation (incarnation) which is adding to the population, but this could subside and we would see a drop in population.

3. How does this theory of the original creation explain all the evidence supporting evolution?

There are two different, but supporting qualities to life. One exists, unchanged. The other is developmental, growing as it experiences. The developing quality was created by the unchanging quality. We call these two qualities: Spirit and Soul. The spirit is simply the life force in its purest nature and it neither began nor does it develop; it simply is, always has been and always will be. The soul quality is like a consciousness within life (spirit) and it does evolve and change as it uses its consciousness and free will, building a complex of memories, attitudes, opinions, etc. In the physical realm of the earth this is manifested in evolution of the physical forms and their minds, but the life force is still just the life force, unchanged from the beginning. Interestingly, there is much speculation that the "missing link" in man's evolutionary process is actually the break between ape evolution which had been tampered with by the companions and the beginning of true physical form for the companions. If you remember in my description of the original creation, there was a point where the companions had bred the apes to a level at which the form was potentially right for "man" to enter, but it needed to make a leap forward that only the original creator could give if it was to be exclusively for the companions. This leap from highly bred ape to first real physical man is quite possibly the missing link.

First of all, there is an association you may want to get in touch with, the Association for Research and Enlightenment.

The A.R.E., as it is called, focuses on the work of Edgar Cayce, but even if you aren't interested in Edgar Cayce's work you'll still find the Association a great resource for your studies. Beyond the Edgar Cayce material the A.R.E. has the best metaphysical library anywhere (you can check out books through the mail if you are a member). They have the most comprehensive mail order book catalog that I've ever seen. Receiving this catalog alone is enough to justify getting in touch with them. The A.R.E. conducts research projects, training courses, lectures, conferences and seminars both at their headquarters in Virginia Beach and in most major cities around the country. These conferences and seminars are not only valuable because of the knowledge they provide, but also because of the many people you can meet who are just as interested in the mysteries of life as you are. The A.R.E. also supports small groups of like-minded people all over this country and in other parts of the world.

To get in touch with this association write to the following address and ask them to send you their book catalog, conference catalog and any information about activities going on in your area. The address is:

A.R.E.
67th St. & Atlantic Ave.
Virginia Beach, VA 23451
(804) 428-3588

RECOMMENDED BOOKS

Here are some key books you may want to read soon. I've organized them by topic and in order of my preference. Most of these books are available for purchase through the A.R.E. book catalog, some can be checked out through their library, and many you may be able to find or order from your local bookstore.

I also recommend you get on the mailing list of InnerVision Publishing Company. You'll receive notices of their latest books on many of the topics below. Their address is:

InnerVision
1218 Eaglewood Drive
Virginia Beach, VA 23454

REINCARNATION—

Reincarnation: The Phoenix Fire Mystery, J. Head and S. L. Cranston, eds. This is a great compilation of the world's thoughts and perceptions on reincarnation. It covers art, literature, philosophy, science and religion, from the East and the West.

KARMA—

Many Mansions, Dr. Gina Cerminara. This is the best book on karma I have ever read. Strongly based on the Edgar Cayce material it gives the most detailed account of how conditions in our present lives are directly related to causes in previous ones.

MEDITATION—

The Secret of the Golden Flower, Translated by Richard Wilhelm and Commentary by C. G. Jung. I've read this book 14 or 15 times and each time something new. It is an ancient Taoist text with illustrations and beautiful descriptions of the inner experiences of meditation.

Meditation: Gateway to Light, Elsie Sechrist. Again, this book is based on the Edgar Cayce

material and is very Christian oriented. It dis-
cusses the spiritual centers, purposes for meditation and how to meditate.

*The Revelation: A Commentary Based on the
Study of Twenty-Four Psychic Discourses by
Edgar Cayce,* Compiled by Members of the
A.R.E. Based on the Edgar Cayce materials
this is an in depth study into the dynamics of
meditation. Many diagrams and charts are used
to help organize the material. I have studied
this book for years and still find it one of the
best. It is a bit difficult, but worth the effort.

Meditation and the Mind of Man, Herbert Puryear, Ph.D. and Mark Thurston, Ph.D. Based
on the Edgar Cayce material, Tibetan and
Taoist techniques and concepts. Very organized and structured, with useful and
practical worksheets and disciplines for you
to use. This book also reviews the purpose
and principals of meditation.

DREAMS

Edgar Cayce on Dreams, Dr. Harmon Bro.
Absolutely the best book I've read on the subject. Harmon's insight into life and the dynam-

115

ics of the dreamer is supported by Edgar Cayce's penetrating vision into the meaning and uses of dreams. I couldn't put it down. When I first read it, I thought I'd never understand my dreams as clearly as Cayce and Bro, but the best interpreter of a dream is truly the dreamer.

God, Dreams and Revelation, Morton Kelsey. Excellent, comprehensive and inspiring. Strongly based on Christianity and the Bible, but with references from other sources as well.

How to Interpret Your Dreams, Mark Thurston, Ph.D. A logical, systematic approach to interpreting your dreams. This is a clear, practical guide with specific steps and methods to follow.

MYSTICISM—

Mysticism, Evelyn Underhill. A classic. It is a study of the nature of man and his awakening spiritual consciousness.

Books & Tapes
from INNER VISION

BOOKS --

☐ BORN AGAIN & AGAIN (Reincarnation), $8.95
by John Van Auken

☐ PAST LIVES & PRESENT RELATIONSHIPS, $8.95
by John Van Auken

☐ DREAMS: In the Life of Prayer & Meditation
An Edgar Cayce Approach, by Harmon Bro, $8.95

☐ GETTING HELP FROM YOUR DREAMS, $9.95
by Henry Reed

☐ DREAM QUEST WORKBOOK, $16.95
by Henry Reed

☐ THE INNER POWER OF SILENCE: A Universal Way
of Meditation, Mark Thurston, $7.95

☐ FATIMA PROPHECY, $9.95
by Ray Stanford

☐ THE SPIRIT UNTO THE CHURCHES (Spiritual Centers
of the Human Body), Ray Stanford, $12.95

☐ THE ADVENTURES OF H. P. (For Children of All Ages)
by Violet Shelley, $5.95

CASSETTE TAPES --

☐ UNDERSTANDING YOUR DREAMS (2-Tape Set), $12.95
by Robert Van de Castle

☐ EDGAR CAYCE'S VISION OF BUILDING A NEW WORLD
(2 Sides), by Harmon Bro, $9.95

☐ PAST LIVES & PRESENT RELATIONSHIPS (2-Tape Set),
by John Van Auken, $14.95

☐ STRESS & BURNOUT (2 Sides), $9.95
by Henry Reed

INNER VISION PUBLISHING CO.
P.O. Box 1117
Virginia Beach, VA 23451

Please send me the books and tapes I have checked. I enclosed a check or
money order for the full amount. I understand that INNER VISION pays all
postage and handling costs. (Allow 4 weeks for delivery.)

☐ Please Send Me Your Free Catalog.

Name _____

Address _____

City _____

State _____ Zip _____